Soul Whispers
of a Corporate Executive

My Legacy to My Kids

Sanjeev Gandhi

Copyright by Sanjeev Gandhi © 2025

All rights reserved.

To Reshma, thank you for providing a colour and texture to my life.

To Sienna and Reiss, this book is for you. Believe in yourself, create incredible memories and be the light this world desperately needs.

To my family and friends, thank you for the unconditional love over the years.

Table of Contents

How to Use This Book:..i
Preface: iii
Life Without the Mask:..iv
Key Quotes From This Book: v

Part I: Foundations of Self & Awareness

Life Is for Living Now:.. 1
Pause. Breathe. Appreciate. 2
I'll Be Happy One Day: 3
FIGJAM – And I'm Not Talking About Jam:... 4
Thoughts / The Power of the Mind: 5
The Gentle Art of Seeing Things as They Are: 6
Guarding Your Energy:... 7
The Power of Choosing Yourself: 8
Love Yourself for What You Truly Are: 9
When Ego Distorts Your Reality: 10
Not Taking Things Personally: 11
The Weight We Give Things: 12
The Power of Thought: 13
Who Are You – Be Honest: 14
Validation of Your Life: 15
Personal Growth Is All Wrong: 16
Self-Discovery in the Age of Distraction:.. 17
Wearing a Mask: 18
The Illusion of Being Present: 19
The Quiet Truth of Purpose: 20
The Reality of Choices Available to You: 21
The Ego of Busyness: 22
Joy Dies in Comparison: 23
Integrity Is Freedom:... 24
Where Compassion Begins – Your Inner Voice:...................................... 25
The Gift Within the Struggle: 26
Suffering is Part of Life:.. 27
Worrying is a Part of Life – "The Fog of War": 28
Travel – Is an Education in Life: 29
Elevate Your Standards: 30
Develop Your Personal Brand: 31
Choose Your Role Models Wisely: 32
Knowledge Is What We Learn; Wisdom Is What We Live:...................... 33
High-Agency Living – Breaking Free from the Herd:............................... 34
Choices and Regrets:.. 35
Even Bad Decisions Can Be Correct Sometimes:.................................... 36
The Power of Effortless Presence:.. 37
How You See the World:... 38
Always Keep Moving Forward:.. 39
Don't Forget – You're a Rare Commodity: 40

Capturing the Moment: 41
Redefining Happiness: 42
The Dance Between Desire, Perception and Rationalisation: 43
Don't Underestimate the Impact of a Compliment: 44
The Power and Philosophy of Saying No: 45
Is It the Journey or the Destination? It's Neither: 46
You Are the Journey: 47
Know Who You Are Today: 48
Gratitude – Your Normal Day is Someone's Dream: 49
Articulating Your Emotions Is Easy: 50
Managing Emotions and Thoughts: 51
Authenticity / Being True to Yourself: 52
Fall in Love With Your Life: 53
Reputation, Character & the Age of Applause: 54
Reputation, Character & the Age of Applause – Part 2: 55
Reflection – Needs to Be Self-Reflective: 56
Becoming the Self You Are Meant to Be: 57
We All Have Good and Bad Days: 58
Self-Care Begins With Self-Truth: 59
The Root of Self-Respect: 60
The Quiet Strength of Self-Sufficiency: 61

Part II: Relationships, Influence & Community

Protect the Family You Build – Always: 63
The Journey of Connection: 64
The Sacred Space of Genuine Care: 65
Until the Lesson Is Learned: 66
Don't Let the Warmth Fade Away: 67
Don't Underestimate Your Sphere of Influence: 68
Reclaiming Power – Boundaries, Truth, and the Narcissist's Illusion: 69
"They Know What They Did" – A Meditation on Silent Boundaries: 70
First Impressions – Be Cautious: 71
Telling People That Their "Baby's Ugly": 72
The Quiet Power of Discretion: 73
Setting Boundaries – The Price of Access: 74
Knowing Where You Stand With People: 75
Having People That Challenge Your Perspective: 76
The Power of Inverse Charisma: 77
The Beauty Within – Instilling Pride in Our Children: 78
Charity Dressed Up as Dignity: 79
You Would be Amazed at How Others See You: 80
Burning Bridges – There Is No Coming Back: 81
Siblings – A Complex Journey of Love and Growth: 82
Energy in Relationships: 83
"All You Need Is Love" by John Lennon – It's a choice to Prioritise Family: ... 84
Love as a Mirror: 85
We Say "Unconditional Love" – But What Do We Mean?: 86

The Most Important Decision in Life:	87
The Invisible Thread Between Two Hearts:	88
Kafka's Beautiful Letters to a Girl:	89
The Truest Form of Love:	90
The Quiet Power of Labels – Yourself and Your Kids:	91
The Heartbreak of a Child is When a Parent Does Not Really Know Them:	92
Your Parents' Voice:	93
Having Children Is Our Second act – First Act Was Ourselves:	94
Parenting in a New Era:	95
Letting Children Become:	96
Reflections on Children – Keeping Them Grounded:	97
The Home You Raise Your Children in Becomes a Part of Their DNA:	98
Do Not Ask Your Kids to Chase Extraordinary Lives:	99
Parenting Beyond Dependence:	100
Re-incarnation or Heaven – Our Children Are Our Afterlife:	101
Peace Over Pressure – Parenting Beyond Outcomes:	102
The Power of Connecting Beyond the Surface:	103
Children – Thank You for the Front Row Seat:	104
True Friendships:	105
Friends of Convenience vs. Friends of Character:	106
The Enduring Power of Friendships:	107
The Truth about Reciprocity and Respect:	108
Finding Your People:	109
Giving People Too Much Attention:	110
Friendship Groups:	111
Your Circle of Friends:	112
High Standards, Small Circles:	113
Be Careful of Your Crowd:	114
The Unexpected Roots of True Support:	115
Respect, Effort, Honesty – Non-Negotiables:	116
Listening – The Heartbeat of Being Human:	117
Disconnected – A Moment Outside of the Noise:	118
Bridging the Gap – From Judgement to Understanding:	119
The Persuasive Paradox – Less Is More:	120
Flattery Is the Easy Option:	121
Why Do People Dislike Others?:	122
The Art of Not Oversharing:	123
A Key Moment in a Friendship:	124
The True Measure of Friendship?:	125

Part III: Growth, Grit & Personal Mastery

The Courage to Actively Live Life:	127
Wanting Is Not Enough:	128
Dreams That Drive You:	129
The Power of Action Over Words:	130
Be Mindful of Your Frequency:	131
You Set Your Own Limits:	132

Embracing Growth – Navigating Unintended Challenges: 133
Not Fulfilling Your Potential Is Terrifying: 134
Taking Accountability of Your Life: 135
Attributes of Great Leaders: 136
People Who Don't Follow the Crowd: 137
Don't Be an Ironing Board: 138
Trapped in the Eyes of Others: 139
The Power of Repetition: 140
The Philosophy of Becoming Exceptional: 141
Success Is a Game – Learn How to Play: 142
Self-Belief – The Great Divider: 143
Being Flexible to Life's External Factors: 144
Mastering a Craft – Finding Your Space in the World: 145
Create First, Perfect Later: 146
The Price of Greatness: 147
Growth – From Ego to Evolution: 148
A Poem – The Curse of Competence: 149
Weathering the Storm – Roger Federer, and the Art of the Moment: 150
Beyond the Hammer – A Philosophy of Perception and Value: 151
Your Future Self: 152
The Price of Authentic Maturity: 153
The Inner Hell of the Unrealised Self: 154
O Captain, My Captain: 155
Ideas in Motion: 156
Stay Fluid, Stay Free: 157
The Trap of Mental Masturbation: 158
The Highest Form of Learning: 159
The Paradox of Effort and Recognition: 160
The Unintended Teachers: 161
The Quiet Power of Compounding: 162
The Long Game – In Praise of the Patient Few: 163
The Power of Focus: 164
Growth Mindset Is Everything: 165
Atomic Habits and the Architecture of Change: 166
Embracing Your Natural Strengths: 167
The Power of Never Giving Up: 168
Leaning In – The Permission Illusion: 169
It's Never Too Late to Begin: 170

Part IV: Society, Illusions & Broader Truths
What You Inspire, They Fear: 172
The Comfort Zone of Being Wrong: 173
Your Multiplicity of Truth: 174
The Truth About Being Special: 175
Life Beyond the Illusion: 176
Empathy – You Don't Know What People Are Going Through: 177
When Did Everything Become Commercial and About Money? 178

Blink and You'll Miss It – The Career Sweet Spot: 179
The Emotion Behind Every Purchase: 180
Be Careful What You Chase: 181
Be Mindful of Your Advice: 182
Before You Criticise Others: 183
Suffering – The Way of the World: 184
The Art of Asking the Right Question: 185
Who Do Smart People Learn From?: 186
What Needs to Change in Society: 187
The "Emperor(s)" in the Executive Suite: 188
Realities of Corporate Life: 189
Success – Understanding the Context of the Game: 190
The Corporate Mirror of the School Drop-off: 191
When Work Becomes Identity: 192
The Price of Love and Costs of Illusion: 193
The World Is Made Up of Two Types of People: 194
Success at What Cost: 195
Nature of Success: 196
Common Lies We Tell Ourselves: 197
The Downside of Success: 198
Rising Above the Game: 199
Functional Depression – Living a Life Behind a Smile: 200
Relaxation for Successful People: 201
Success Without Soul Is Failure: 202
Stop Worrying – It's All Immaterial in the Long Term: 203
The Fragility of Trust: 204
When Morality Becomes Personal: 205
Competition vs. Collaboration: 206
Curiosity – The Key to Inner Doors: 207
What Is Normal to You… May Not Be Normal to Others: 208
Be Careful Not to Chase Illusions: 209
The Price of Privilege: 210
Status Games – The Game of Insecurity: 211
When Enough is Never Enough: 212
The New Normal – A Quiet Tragedy: 213
The Puzzle of Life: 214

Part V: Wealth, Freedom & Long-Term Thinking
A Life Worth Looking Back On: 216
Time – The Here and Now: 217
The Paradox of Presence and Loss: 218
The Meaning Can Only Be Found in Doing the Thing: 219
The Power of Awe: 220
The True Meaning of Financial Freedom: 221
Work – Are You Climbing the Right Mountain: 222
The Texture of a Winning Life: 223
Success Is a Direct Reflection of Effort: 224

Words That Change Lives: 225
Limits on Wealth – What Money Cannot Buy: 226
Best Time to Do Anything: 227
Making Change Happen: 228
Modern Day Laziness – Being Busy: 229
Wealth Is Freedom, Not Acquisition: 230
The Paycheque Cage: 231
Money Is a Means, Freedom Is the Goal: 232
Money, Work, and Influence – The Pareto Effect: 233
Money Magnifies Who You Truly Are: 234
The Quiet Grace of the Working Life: 235
Currency of Life: 236
The Red Car Theory – Where Attention Goes Reality Follows: 237
Greed – When is Enough Enough?: 238
No Such Thing as a Free Lunch: 239
Health – The Most Important Lesson in Life: 240
Investing for the Future Takes Patience: 241
The Power of Choosing How We See the World: 242
The Greatest Freedom: 243
Following Your Passions: 244
The Power of Embracing "Enough": 245
Without Health You Have Nothing: 246
Every Genius Has Its Own Path: 247

Part VI: Meaning, Spirit & Inner Strength
Understanding Life – John Lennon's Experience: 249
Our Ancestors – We Walk On Their Strength: 250
The Power Within – Choosing Your Story: 251
The Pulse of the Crowd, The Meaning of Life: 252
The Sacred Truths of Being Human: 253
From Craving to Gratitude – The Journey of Valuing: 254
Karma as Choice, Not Judgement: 255
The Strength of a Gentle Soul: 256
Definition of Real Beauty: 257
Be the Change – The Quiet Power of Small Acts: 258
No Man Walks in the Same River Twice: 259
The Quiet Power of Forgiveness: 260
The Power of Your Imagination: 261
Joy Without Reason: 262
The Eulogy We Write Each Day: 263
Strength in Vulnerability and Restraint: 264
"Drowning Child" – The Moral Duty to Help: 265
Self-Confidence – The Irrefutable Definition: 266
Turning a Mid-Life Into the Pivotal Years: 267
Living Amongst Dreams Made Real: 268
Beyond Comfort – The Beauty of a Life Well Lived: 269
The Privilege of Everyday Life: 270

Perspective Is a Strange Thing: 271
Perspective & Judgement: 272
Life's Direction: 273
Reframing for Gratitude – The Greatest Privilege: 274
Appreciate Your Loved Ones – The Inner Dialogue We Dread Will Come: 275
Destiny and the Illusion of Choice: 276
Time – The Sweetness of Doing Nothing: 277
Time Is Your Most Valuable Asset: 278
Time – The Invisible Account: 279
4,000 Weeks to Live – Make Them Count: 280
When What We Do Outshadows What We Become: 281
Life's Lessons on Anger: 282
The Last Refuge for Creativity – You Will Not See Showers the Same Again:283
The Power of Music – It Stirs Emotions: 284
No Moment Is Truly Mundane: 285
Living For the Future Is a Wasted Life: 286
The Future or Are We Already There? 287
Failure and People's Perception: 288
Death – An Inspirational Perspective: 289
The Answer is Not in Fulfilling Your Dreams: 290
We See You, We're Proud of You: 291

Part VII: Final Reflections ....
Getting Older Is Strange and Beautiful: 293
A Life Built in Stillness: 294
Living an Unfulfilled Life – Impacts Your Kids: 295
Getting Old – Living Forward With Intention: 296
If You Knew You Were Going to Die One Year from Today: 297
How to Stop Ageing: 298
Embrace Life's Unscripted Moments: 299
Definition of Happiness: 300
Why Does Happiness Elude Successful People?: 301
Success Is Not What You've Been Told: 302
Be Truthful to Yourself: 303
A Beautiful Life Includes Hope: 304
Things Happen When They Are Meant to Happen: 305
Showing Up – The Language of True Humanity: 306
A Beautiful Life Is Poetry in Motion: 307
Learning to Die Peacefully: 308

How to Use This Book:

Soul Whispers of a Corporate Executive is a deeply personal and philosophical reflection, offering timeless wisdom through the lens of a seasoned corporate leader.

As a legacy to his children, the book invites readers to dip into its insights whenever they need guidance or inspiration. Its beauty lies in its structure – an anthology of "aha moments" collected over three decades, drawn from both the professional world and moments of quiet introspection.

The book encourages regular revisits, as the right philosophical wisdom may speak to readers at different points in their lives, offering fresh perspectives when needed most. Though rooted in the experiences of a corporate executive, the messages transcend business, focusing instead on living a virtuous life, appreciating the texture of everyday moments, and embracing personal growth.

It's not just a book to read; it's a resource for reflection, offering the kind of insight that stays with you, whether read in its entirety or savoured in small bursts over time.

It also presents a great opportunity to spark meaningful conversations – perfect for dinner parties where one can open to a random page, read a passage aloud, and ask guests whether they agree with the reflection. This unique approach invites deeper dialogue, shared introspection, and connection among friends, colleagues, or even strangers.

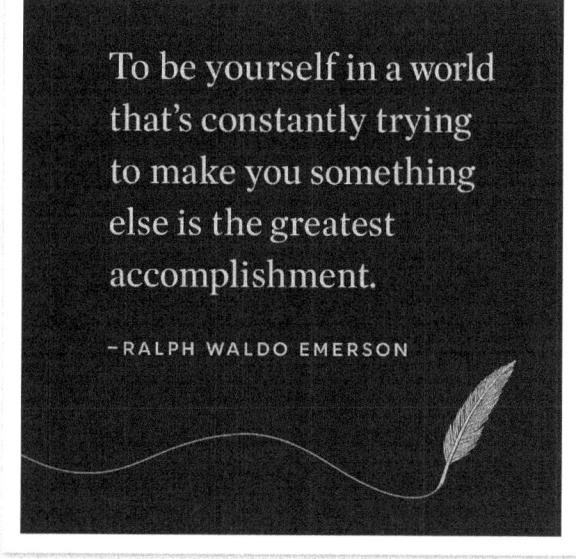

Preface:

This book, *Soul Whispers of a Corporate Executive* is my legacy – a collection for my children to dip in and out of during their lives.

It focuses on: the essential truths, appreciating the texture of everyday life, and reflections on how to live with virtue. Many of these topics are neither discussed nor taught in the modern world but left for individuals to discover for themselves as part of their own journey of personal growth.

The genesis of this book is as Naval Ravikant once said: *"Inspiration is perishable."*

So what I have collated, are things I have heard, seen, discussed that inspired me. These items may not resonate at a specific time but I invite you to revisit them regularly. At the right time and under the right context, the right philosophical doctrine will jump out and have a material impact.

I am proud to say that I have conscientiously kept a note of all of these "aha moments" over the past 30 years.

This is truly my life's work.

Life Without the Mask:

After having spent decades in Leadership and Executive teams, travelling the world for business, working across three time zones, and averaging over 70 hours a week, I now find myself in a new phase of my life that I am coining **"my second mountain."**

When you don't have to worry about paying bills, or showing up to a "9-to-5," you gain time to be present – and think. The system isn't designed for most to ever reach this level. But here, in this quiet, I can see things more clearly. It also allows me to tap into passions and unfulfilled potential.

Fundamentally, there are three aspects to my journey:

1. Letting go of my identity allows me to be set free. Years of clinging to my identity as a professional forced me to play a role and hold onto behaviours that served me, yes, but which stopped me from showing my true self. The concern for me was that **"if you wear the mask long enough it becomes the face." (Oscar Wilde)**

2. I'm now unravelling everything and everyone that no longer aligns with where I am. Today, I value integrity, honesty, and authenticity above all else in the people and things I invest time in.

3. I no longer seek "a purpose." For much of my life, purpose was 'something I had to have' to allow me to save face with the world. But now, there are no special missions and no great discoveries of oneself… **I have no face left to save.**

Letting go – of my identity, of chasing money, of striving to "find my purpose" and of the need to explain this all to others – has allowed me to live life more effortlessly. My ego has been set free!

Because purpose isn't something you *find, achieve or become*… it's something you embody every day… I've also found myself comfortable being unapologetically protective of MY needs and MY wants!

I've invested considerable time and energy into understanding myself, clarifying my thoughts, and breaking free from the past. I now fully appreciate the costs I've paid but what I can't forget are my past experiences, the memories created, friendships forged and most importantly, the person it allowed me to become.

In short: my focus now is to move forward consciously and mindfully – while also celebrating the sweetness of doing nothing.

This is my time.

Key Quotes From This Book:

"Life will present itself as an external game. How you succeed is based on how you turn it into an internal one."

"The privilege of a lifetime is to become who you truly are and not what you have achieved."
– Carl Jung

"You once dreamt of the life you have now. If you don't like your life now, you are also unlikely to like the life you dream of now!"

"You spend the first 30 years building your character. That character then determines your future and legacy."

"Never forget – things don't happen to you, they happen for you."
– Tony Robbins

"Winners define themselves by what they made happen, losers define themselves by what happened to them."

"My diet is not just what I eat, it's also what I read, who I spend time with, what I watch, etc."

Part I: Foundations of Self & Awareness

Themes: Identity, Presence, Purpose, Mindfulness

Life Is for Living Now:

Pause. Breathe. Appreciate.

In a world that rushes forward, it is a radical act to pause. To breathe. To simply appreciate.

Gratitude is not just a feeling – it is a form of awareness, a quiet rebellion against the urge to constantly seek more. It is the art of seeing the sacred in the ordinary.

Appreciate the warmth of the sun on your skin – proof that you are alive and held by the same light that nourishes all things.

Appreciate a stranger's smile – an unspoken reminder that connection can exist without words.

Appreciate the people who say, "I care about you," because in a fleeting world, such honesty is a gift.

Appreciate the effort others make for you – not for what it gives you, but for what it says about their heart.

Appreciate the pride in your chest when you do what once seemed impossible – it is a sign that you are growing beyond your limits.

Appreciate the small victories, the new skills, the quiet moments of becoming.

Appreciate the smiles that come unprovoked, like laughter from the soul.

Appreciate the truth that you are not finished – you are a work in progress, sculpted by time, shaped by experience.

And most of all, appreciate this:

> **"You have yet to meet the person you're destined to become."**

I'll Be Happy One Day:

I'll be happy...

...when I grow up

...when I get a job

...when I retire

...when I...

"If you can't be happy enjoying your coffee now, you will never be happy owning a yacht in the future – stop chasing rainbows!"

– Naval Ravikant

FIGJAM – And I'm Not Talking About Jam:

FIGJAM stands for: F--- I'm Good, Just Ask Me.

These are the moments that don't earn you applause, the quiet victories where no one else notices, but you know.

It's those times when you accomplish something – big or small – and you feel an internal glow. There's no external validation, no credit from others, but you stand there, quietly proud of what you've done. You may not hear the applause, but at that moment, you're your own biggest fan.

These are the moments where you give yourself a pat on the back, even if no one else sees the effort behind it. It's a personal recognition of your strength, your growth, your progress – whether anyone else knows or not.

Keep a note of those moments, and every so often, you'll catch yourself smiling. They remind you of how far you've come, even if the world hasn't noticed yet.

"FIGJAMs give you that confidence to keep going and do better."

Thoughts / The Power of the Mind:

Be careful of your thoughts...

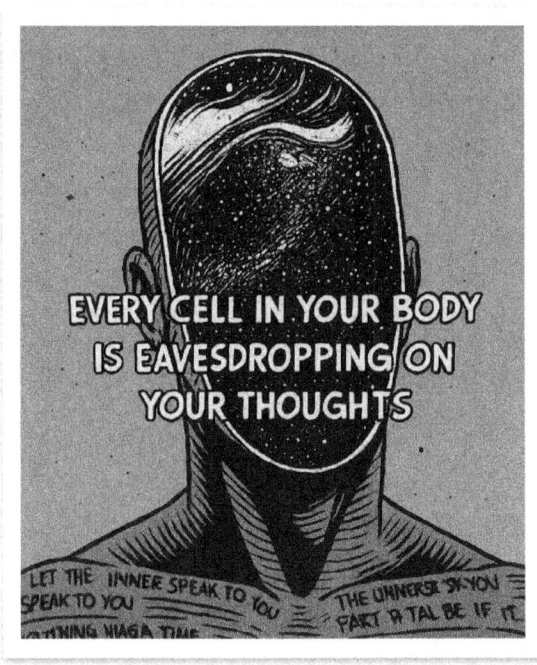

The Gentle Art of Seeing Things as They Are:

There is an extraordinary power in simply observing things for what they are – not through the lens of judgement, resistance, or expectation, but with a deep and compassionate presence. True understanding begins not with control, but with love. *"I must love the very thing I am studying."* For without love, we reduce what we observe to something to be fixed or resisted, rather than something to be truly known.

If you want to understand a child, you cannot do so by correcting every flaw or silencing every outburst. You must *watch*, with tenderness. You must enter their world – not as a critic, but as a witness. To see how they move, how they think, how they carry their wonder and fears. And only then, when you have let go of your urge to mould them, can you truly begin to know them. This is not just about children – it's about life, about ourselves, about everything.

To understand *what is*, you must allow it to *be*. Whether it is your own anger, your joy, your confusion, or your desire – you must observe it without immediate need to correct or judge. *That* is the actual. That is where transformation begins. Not through force, but through awareness. Not by running from discomfort, but by sitting beside it, gently.

There is great humility in this practice. It asks us to relinquish our desire to control and instead cultivate curiosity. It asks us to replace condemnation with compassion. In doing so, we begin to see the world – not as we wish it to be – but as it truly is. And in that raw, unfiltered seeing, something miraculous happens: understanding takes root, and with it, a quiet kind of freedom.

Guarding Your Energy:

Learn the art of observing without absorbing. Your energy is precious – protect it.

How do we do this when we're among others? By choosing carefully who we let close, and by setting gentle boundaries. Not every presence deserves a place in our inner world.

Why does this matter? Because the company we keep shapes our peace. Surrounding ourselves with kindness and support nourishes the soul, while negativity weighs it down.

Maturity, then, is this: the wisdom to recognise what energy we welcome and the courage to take responsibility for our own well-being.

It is the quiet strength of knowing that what we allow in shapes who we become.

The Power of Choosing Yourself:

There's a moment when you stand at the crossroads. One path: worn smooth by compromise. The other: wild, untamed, and yours alone.

This is where you decide: will you keep living for everyone else? Or will you finally choose yourself?

But here's the truth no one tells you:

> *"Choosing what's important to you hurts."*

It means walking away from people and places you swore you'd hold onto forever. It means letting go of dreams that don't fit anymore, even when they still feel like home. It means stepping into a version of you that terrifies you because you've never met them before.

But do you know what hurts more? Staying, shrinking, compromising who you are and living a life that was never really yours.

The power of choosing yourself isn't just about what you gain. It's about what you release:

- The weight of trying to be everything for everyone
- The chains of other people's expectations
- The suffocating need to prove you're worthy.

When you choose yourself, you start declaring:

"I am and have everything I need. I set the standard for who and what enters my life!"

Love Yourself for What You Truly Are:

When Ego Distorts Your Reality:

In essence, ego-driven stories are mental patterns or beliefs that shape our identity and emotional reactions.

While some stories help us navigate life, others can trap us in limiting or false views of ourselves and reality. The ego can be deceptive. It can pretend to speak truth but often leads us into illusion. It tells stories not to free us, but to protect its fragile sense of self.

Much of that imagined suffering comes from the ego's need to tell comforting, self-serving stories.

The ego doesn't care about truth – it cares about consistency. It convinces us we're victims when we're just facing challenges. It calls us heroes when we're just lucky. It needs us to feel special, because the idea of being ordinary feels threatening.

Epictetus put it well:

> *"It is not things themselves that disturb us, but our opinions about them."*

And most opinions are just stories we tell ourselves. Others will also turn you into whatever fits their story – villain, saviour, fool. It's not personal. It's just how people make sense of the world. You don't need to correct their version or prove your side. Let go of the need to be understood.
Silence the ego long enough to see reality clearly – without needing to be right, admired, or justified.

Freedom isn't in controlling the story.

It's in no longer needing one.

Not Taking Things Personally:

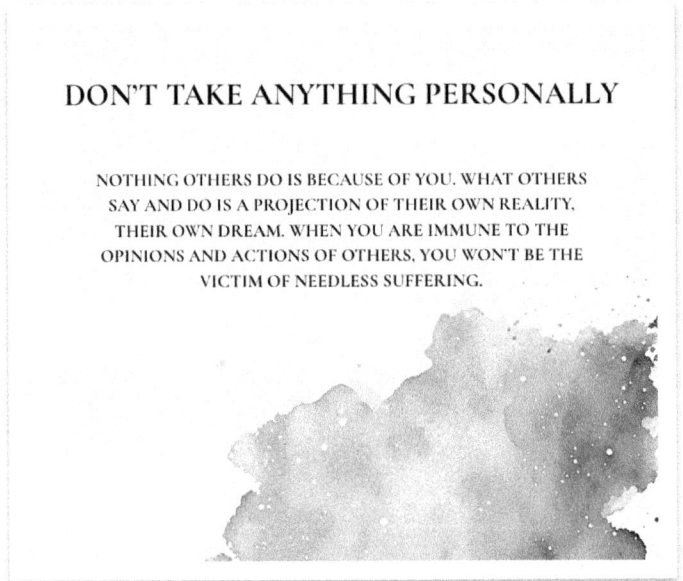

The Weight We Give Things:

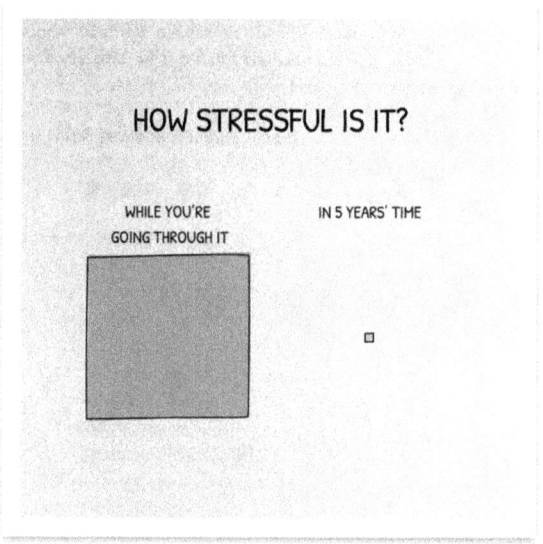

Stress arises when we lose the present moment, placing the future above the life unfolding now. Yet, over time, what once seemed urgent and troubling often fades in importance. The things we worry over rarely hold the weight we give them.

As Marcus Aurelius reminds us,

"If you are distressed by anything external, the pain is not due to the thing itself, but to your estimate of it; and this you have the power to revoke at any moment."

The Power of Thought:

"Whether you think you can, or whether you think you can't – you're right!"

– Henry Ford

Who Are You – Be Honest:

Who are you when no one is watching? When you are alone with just your thoughts, your actions, and no one to answer to?

Take a moment and think about the times when you're in your car – a place where you are free from the expectations of others.

No partner beside you. No children in the backseat. No friends chatting away. No parents observing your every move.

In those moments of solitude, how do you act?

Are you calm and composed?

Are you courteous to other drivers, respecting the flow of the world around you?

Or do you find yourself swearing at others, feeling frustrated by the smallest inconvenience?

Perhaps you toss that empty wrapper out the window or forget the very idea of civility because, after all, no one is watching.

In the silence of your car, away from the eyes of others, the truth of your character often reveals itself. It's easy to act kind when others are looking, but who are you when no one is paying attention? That is the true reflection of your inner self.

Your actions in those quiet moments say more than words ever could.

So, who are you – really?

– Inspired by Jimmy Carr

Validation of Your Life:

Personal Growth Is All Wrong:

Self-improvement seems to be the term of the day right now but are we improving on areas that really count?

In *Meditations,* Marcus Aurelius talks about improving on his hobby (which happened to be Roman wrestling) but what he struggled with was where did he put time aside in becoming:

- A better friend
- A more forgiving person
- A more charitable human
- A humbler individual
- A better human for society at large

i.e. the things that are not immediately visible or measurable.

As Marcus Aurelius posits, our personal growth journey needs to focus on those attributes that can ripple into a better society.

What will you focus on?

– Inspired by Ryan Holiday in the Daily Stoic

Self-Discovery in the Age of Distraction:

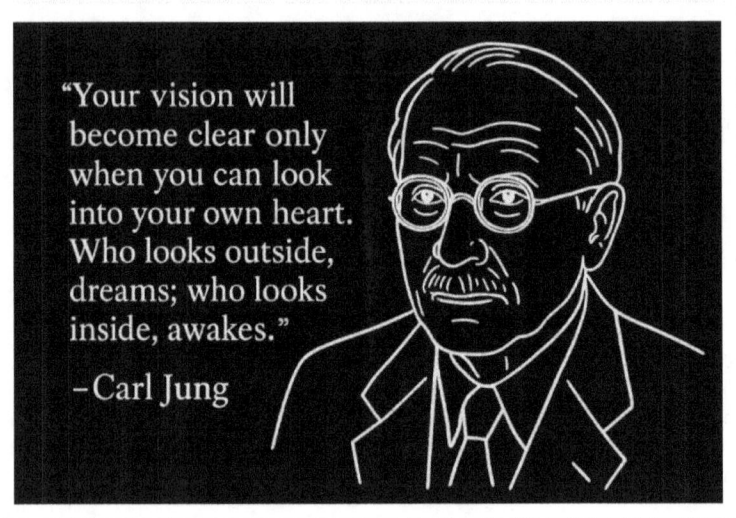

To "look outside" is to live in abstraction, projecting desires onto a world that can never fully satisfy the soul. We dream of who we might be, shaped by comparisons and expectations. But to "look inside" is to awaken – to confront the hidden architecture of our fears, hopes, and contradictions. This inner gaze leads to authenticity, self-integration, and ultimately, peace.

In modern times, Jung's message is not a retreat from the world, but a return to the self – the only place where consciousness deepens, and the human spirit is truly known.

Wearing a Mask:

As you grow, you realize it's better to put a mask on, so as to be liked and get certain things you want.

A fake smile, a popular opinion, tacit approval on situations you disagree with.

The problem appears when you wear that mask for too long; you think the mask is your face.

The Illusion of Being Present:

"Most people are worried about not being here (i.e. dying) but are so distracted in life they are not here in the moment anyway."

– Thich Nhat Hanh

The relevance of this insight couldn't be greater today. We've built a culture that rewards multitasking, idolises productivity, and often equates busyness with worth.

We fear death, yet rarely notice how often we abandon life while still breathing. In our attempt to preserve existence, we forget to experience it. We spend our days racing toward an imagined future, all the while missing the only thing that ever truly exists: the present moment.

Modern life is a paradox. We have created a culture that exalts productivity and glorifies the ability to juggle many things at once, as though scattering our attention were a virtue. The more we do, the more we are praised. But in trying to be everywhere, we end up being nowhere at all.

In the name of success, we disconnect – from our own thoughts, from the people we love, from the quiet pulse of life happening right now. We check emails during conversations, plan tomorrow during dinner, and scroll through other people's lives while our own quietly passes us by.

To be present is not just a lifestyle change – it is a philosophical act. It is to choose awareness over autopilot, depth over distraction. It is to resist the illusion that life is something to be managed, and instead to see it as something to be lived.

To live well is not merely to avoid death, but to inhabit our days with full presence. In every breath, every conversation, every unnoticed miracle of being alive – there lies the truth we spend a lifetime seeking.

The Quiet Truth of Purpose:

The ego, ever restless, seeks to define itself through action – its impulse is to *do*. The heart, in contrast, seeks not to act but to *be*. In its stillness, it already knows what the ego is striving to find.

The ego murmurs, *"Once you discover your purpose, then you will be fulfilled."* Yet this is the great illusion: that purpose is a distant summit to be reached, rather than a truth quietly residing in the present moment.

Purpose is not a destination on the map of becoming – it is a return to the essence of being. One does not need to *find* it, only to unburden the mind of the idea that it lies somewhere ahead, waiting in the shadows of future accomplishments.

It was never concealed in a grand task or a noble mission. Purpose reveals itself in the simple act of living with love, in the sincerity of each breath, in the presence we bring to ordinary moments.

There are no epic quests required. No self to be *found*, only a self to be *remembered*.

To believe one's purpose lies in doing something "great" is to place conditions upon what is already whole. In this striving, we obscure the truth that *we are already enough*.

When I release the compulsion to define or perform my purpose, I begin to live it – effortlessly, authentically.

For purpose is not a prize to be earned, nor a role to be played. It is the quiet radiance of being itself.

The Reality of Choices Available to You:

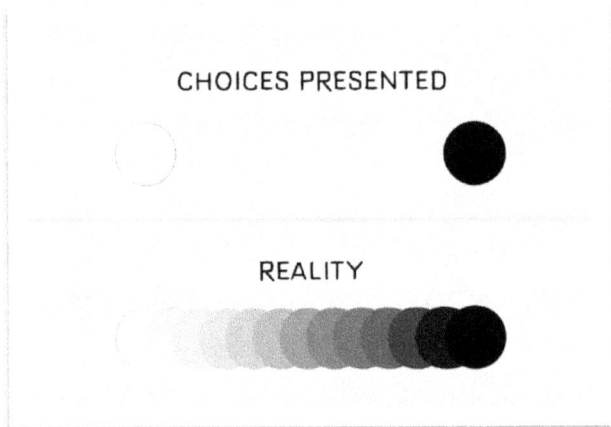

Life rarely presents us with only the clear-cut choices laid before us. More often, reality offers a spectrum of possibilities that lie between, beyond, or even outside the given options. The world is not limited to either/or decisions – there are blends, alternatives, and creative paths that can be shaped by your values, imagination, and circumstances.

Recognising this requires stepping back, questioning what's truly available, and realising that the freedom to choose often includes the freedom to redefine the choices themselves.

The Ego of Busyness:

"How are you today?" It's something I ask often, just like everyone else. And yet, how often do I hear the response, "Busy?"

It used to be that I'd respond the same way, *"Busy"*, as if it were the only answer that made sense. I caught myself doing it more times than I'd like to admit. Busyness had become my identity, my validation. The more I did, the more important I felt – or so I thought. It's easy to fall into the trap, isn't it?

But then, I started to wonder: When did "busy" become a response at all? Why is it the first thing that comes out of our mouths when asked how we're doing? Isn't it supposed to be about how we *feel* – not just a laundry list of tasks and obligations?

The truth is, "busy" became my ego speaking, not my soul. It was a way to show that I had value, that my time mattered, that I was somehow accomplishing something meaningful. But here's the thing I realised – being busy doesn't always mean being productive. And sometimes, it's just a distraction from what really matters.

Now, when someone asks me, "How are you today?" I try to stop myself before I give that autopilot answer. Instead of rushing to say, "I'm busy," I try to take a moment to reflect. Am I *really* busy, or am I just filling my days because it's easier than sitting with stillness?

I think the most important thing I've learned is that being busy isn't a reflection of worth. It's just noise. So, I've started asking myself: Am I truly present? Am I finding moments to breathe, to simply be?

It's easy to fall into the trap of busyness. But I've learned that *being* – really being, without the need to justify myself with productivity – is what really makes life rich. And I don't want to lose sight of that again.

Joy Dies in Comparison:

Comparison in anything kills all joy.

Be careful, live your own life.

Integrity Is Freedom:

Integrity – is the foundation of everything

Integrity comes from the Latin word *integritas*, meaning "one" or "whole." People who are one way on the inside and another way on the outside – i.e., not "whole" – lack integrity; they have "duality" instead.

While presenting your view as something other than what it is can sometimes be easier in the moment (because you can avoid conflict, or embarrassment, or achieve some other short-term goal), the second – and third-order effects of having integrity and avoiding duality are immense. People who are one way on the inside and another on the outside become conflicted and often lose touch with their own values. It's difficult for them to be happy and almost impossible for them to be their best.

Aligning what you say, with what you think, and what you think, with what you feel, will make you much happier and much more successful.

Thinking solely about what's accurate instead of how it is perceived pushes you to focus on the most important things.

It helps you sort through people and places because you'll be drawn to people and places that are open and honest. It's also fairer to those around you: Making judgements about people so that they are tried and sentenced.

Where Compassion Begins – Your Inner Voice:

There is a voice inside you, quiet yet constant – the one that narrates your choices, judges your missteps, and sometimes forgets to offer the same kindness it extends so easily to others. We are taught, from childhood, to treat others as we wish to be treated. This golden rule shines with moral clarity – a call to empathy, fairness, compassion. Yet we often forget the reverse: to treat ourselves as kindly as we treat those we love.

For many, the inner voice becomes a harsh critic, a perfectionist, a shadow that never quite forgives. It holds us to standards we'd never impose on a friend. Where we would reassure others, we reproach ourselves. Where we would listen gently, we demand silently. It is a strange hypocrisy, to show mercy outward but withhold it inward.

This inner relationship – the ongoing dialogue between who we are and how we speak to ourselves – must be nurtured like any other. It is not weakness to offer yourself grace; it is wisdom. Compassion toward the self is not self-indulgence, but the soil in which authentic empathy grows. A person who can befriend their own voice becomes stronger, more resilient, more whole.

So speak to yourself with the tone you reserve for someone you truly care for. Correct when needed, but forgive just as quickly. Listen with patience. Encourage rather than condemn. The voice inside you becomes the foundation of your world – make it a place worth living in.

The Gift Within the Struggle:

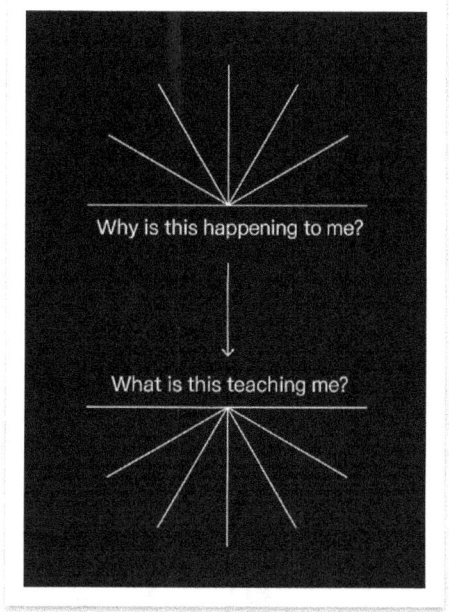

"Things happen for you and not to you."

– Tony Robbins

This one line has allowed me to elevate my thoughts.

While difficult experiences and setbacks may often feel like they're imposed on you, they ultimately serve a purpose and contribute to your growth and development in ways you can't immediately see.

It encourages a mindset of viewing challenges as opportunities and seeking lessons and silver linings in adversity.

Nothing is wasted.

Everything is working for you.

Suffering is Part of Life:

Worrying is a Part of Life – "The Fog of War":

Worry is woven into the very fabric of our existence – like the relentless fog that clouds the battlefield of life. This "fog of war" is not just uncertainty about the external world, but a deeper, trembling doubt within ourselves: about our strength, our choices, our unfolding path. It is the murmur of fear whispering through the unknown.

Yet, this fog is part of being human. It envelops us in moments of hesitation, anxiety, and restless questioning.

And here lies the paradox: when we peer back through the lens of time, the haze begins to lift. What once seemed impenetrable confusion reveals itself as clarity, insight, and understanding.

Worry, then, is both a burden and a teacher – a shadow that veils the present but also a signpost that we are alive, engaged, and growing. To live fully is to accept the fog without surrendering to it, to trust that beyond the uncertainty lies a truth that only time can unveil.

Travel – Is an Education in Life:

Elevate Your Standards:

Not everything that entertains, pleases, or attracts us is beneficial.

Just because something tastes good, looks appealing, or feels enjoyable in the moment doesn't mean it aligns with what's truly good for us.

In a world full of distractions and instant gratification, it's essential to walk with a higher level of discernment, wisdom, and purpose. This requires pausing, reflecting, and choosing what nourishes us in the long term, rather than simply satisfying fleeting desires.

When we elevate our standards, we protect our time, energy, and growth, ensuring that what we bring into our lives adds lasting value, not just temporary pleasure.

> **High standards protect you from low quality experiences.**

Develop Your Personal Brand:

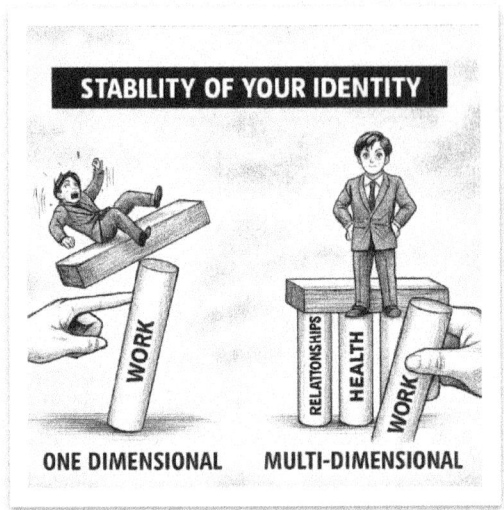

The foundation of a strong personal brand starts with tying your identity to your own name, not your job title, possessions, or relationships. Remember this: who you are is your most valuable asset – and it's the one thing no one can take from you.

Many people build their identity around external markers like being a doctor, a lawyer, investment banker, a wealthy person's child, or someone's partner. But those roles can change or disappear. When your self-worth is wrapped up in things that can be lost or something that undermines who you are, you're standing on shaky ground.

Instead, anchor your brand in your character, values, passions and name. This will instil a level of confidence in you that is unshakeable. Let the world know what you stand for, not just what you do. That's how you build self-confidence and something real, lasting, and truly yours.

Choose Your Role Models Wisely:

Not everyone who rides a horse is a jockey! Who you look up to and take advice from can define your success.

In a world obsessed with wealth, fame, and visibility, we often mistake loud success for deep wisdom. But who you choose to admire, who you seek advice from, quietly shapes the path you walk and the values you carry.

Look beyond millionaires and moguls. Look to the patient father, the wise mother, the teacher who gives without asking, the friend who shows up when no one is watching. True role models are not defined by what they've accumulated, but by what they've cultivated – character, humility, consistency, and kindness.

And most importantly, choose role models who are close enough to touch – just one or two rungs above you. Someone whose life you can reasonably reach for, whose journey lights a path rather than casts a shadow. When the gap is too wide, admiration turns into disempowerment.

Who you ask for guidance matters. Choose those whose values echo the life you want to live. Because sometimes, the greatest wisdom comes not from those who have everything, but from those who have learned to value the right things.

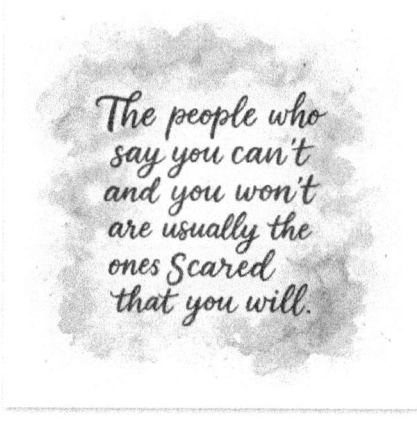

The people who say you can't and you won't are usually the ones scared that you will.

Knowledge Is What We Learn; Wisdom Is What We Live:

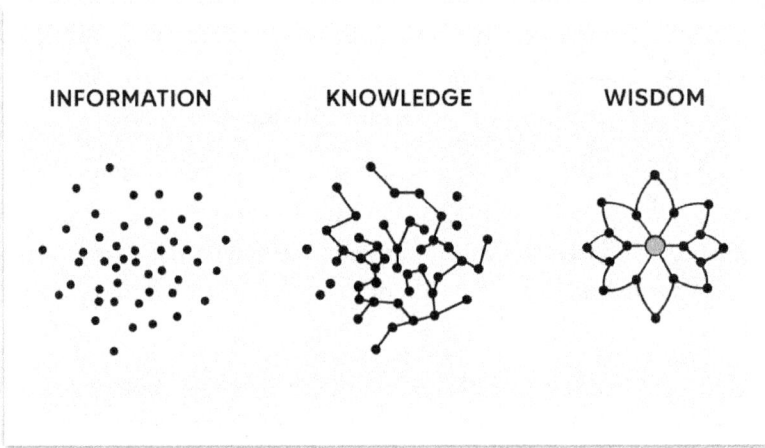

Knowledge is the accumulation of facts, information, and skills that we gain through learning and experience. It's about what we know. Wisdom, on the other hand, is the deeper understanding of how to apply that knowledge thoughtfully and judiciously in real life.

It involves insight, good judgement, and the ability to navigate complex situations with perspective and compassion. While knowledge can be taught, wisdom is often earned through reflection and experience.

As mentioned, wisdom is the deeper insight – knowing when and how to apply that knowledge, like recognising that a tomato, despite being a fruit, does not belong in a fruit salad.

High-Agency Living – Breaking Free from the Herd:

Ask yourself: Are you a passenger in life's journey, or the captain steering your own course?

Those who embody true agency do not drift with the crowd but chart their own way. They are grounded in trustworthiness and clarity of mind, wielding resourcefulness and tenacity as their tools. They act with urgency, not out of haste, but from a deep commitment to purposeful action.

To live with high agency is to reclaim your power – to move beyond the passive flow of circumstance and instead shape your reality with intention and courage. It is the quiet rebellion of choosing authenticity over conformity, wisdom over convenience. In this choice lies freedom – the freedom to be the author of your own life.

Are you the person in picture A or picture B?

Choices and Regrets:

Choices are the act of choosing between two or more possibilities.

Regret often isn't about the choice you made but about the stories we tell ourselves about how it could have been different – yet those alternate realities are just illusions.

The truth is, even if you had made different choices, there's no guarantee things would have turned out better; they might have led to new forms of pain or different kinds of loss.

Understanding that regret is often about mourning a fantasy rather than an actual possibility can help you release the grip of "what if" and find peace in accepting the "what is."

Healing begins when you realise that the past could never have been as perfect as you imagined, and perhaps, where you are now is exactly where you were meant to be.

Even Bad Decisions Can Be Correct Sometimes:

"Even a broken clock is correct twice a day."

Sometimes, what appears as a mistake may still hold truth.

Like a broken clock that aligns with time twice a day, even wrong choices can reveal moments of correctness. Life's complexity reminds us that error and insight often coexist, urging us to embrace imperfection as part of wisdom.

The Power of Effortless Presence:

"Act with the presence of rarefied air and effortless superiority!"

– Inspired by a philosophy used within a leading professional services firm.

You can always tell when someone is destined for success because they are unmistakably different – without even trying. Their demeanour, energy, and presence simply *are*.

This effortless presence is not an act but a reflection of deep authenticity and inner confidence. In a world that constantly pressures you to become someone else, cultivating this grounded sense of self is an act of quiet rebellion.

Authenticity paired with inner confidence leads to a divine order – a rhythm of life where success flows naturally, without struggle or noise.

As Rumi said,

"Wherever you stand, be the soul of that place!"

To live with such presence is to embody a power beyond achievement, a timeless strength found in simply *being*.

How You See the World:

"Your living is determined not so much by what life brings to you as by the attitude you bring to life; not so much by what happens to you as by the way your mind looks at what happens."

– Khalil Gibran

Manifestation seems to be the buzzword of the moment.

One of the biggest challenges I see in those hoping to manifest success is that they only focus on what they want as an outcome.

People need to spend more time being specific in what they are imagining who they will be. How they will face obstacles and handle insecurities. They need to figure out how they want to show up – what characteristics and skills they will have invested time and hard work developing and nurturing.

People also need to think that what they are doing now needs to change. People are not going to become significantly more successful by being more productive i.e. answering more emails, working harder etc., you need to move out of being an operator to becoming an ideas person, a leader – someone whose presence determines their value as opposed to someone doing things.

Always Keep Moving Forward:

> Rumi said,
>
> "As you start to walk on the way, the way appears."
>
> Clarity doesn't come before action, it comes from action.

Don't Forget – You're a Rare Commodity:

"Learn to act with effortless superiority and a rarefied air – embody your uniqueness!"

Capturing the Moment:

> "DON'T LEAVE ANYTHING FOR LATER.
> LATER, THE COFFEE GETS COLD. LATER, YOU LOSE INTEREST.
> LATER, THE DAY TURNS INTO NIGHT.
> LATER, PEOPLE GROW OLD.
> LATER, LIFE GOES BY.
> LATER, YOU REGRET NOT DOING SOMETHING... WHEN YOU HAD THE CHANCE."
> —TOSHIKAZU KAWAGUCHI

Redefining Happiness:

Happiness is not in the perfection of your surroundings, but in the depth of love shared within them. It's not about achieving goals by a certain age or hitting predefined milestones; rather, it's about being present – fully immersing yourself in the moments that make up your life. True happiness isn't dependent on the approval of others, but in waking up every morning at peace with yourself, excited for the day ahead, and grounded in the present moment, unconcerned with how you are perceived.

It's not about having the finest things in life, but about making the best of what you have right now. Happiness is knowing you've given your best with what you've been given, without waiting for everything to fall perfectly into place.

It's in the silver linings, the quiet moments that remind you that no matter the chaos around you, the light is always there, patiently waiting for you to notice.

Happiness isn't a destination – it's a way of seeing, being, and living. It's a choice to find joy in the journey, even when the road is imperfect, and to savour the present with a heart that is open and alive.

The Dance Between Desire, Perception and Rationalisation:

Living in this day and age is fascinating as everyone is so desperate to be flavour of the month, they all want to be seen at the newest in-places, they want to drive a certain car brand etc. – social media may have a hand in this. Notwithstanding this, when you speak to them it's so interesting to see how they reframe and rationalise their specific situation. It's laughable at times!

In the Aesop's fable, "The Fox and the Grapes," the fox, unable to reach the luscious grapes, convinces himself they are sour. This tale illustrates a psychology where individuals adjust their beliefs to align with their experiences, often to preserve self-esteem. Rather than confronting the pain of unattainable desires, we might devalue them, asserting they were unworthy from the start. This defence mechanism, while protective, can hinder personal growth by preventing honest self-assessment.

By acknowledging these psychological patterns, we can have greater self-awareness, embrace both our aspirations and our limitations with honesty and grace. Not lying to ourselves is at the heart of being authentic.

Don't Underestimate the Impact of a Compliment:

A single compliment, though small in form, holds the potential to ignite a profound transformation.

When genuinely offered, it affirms a person's worth, often in ways they didn't know they needed. This simple act of recognition can pierce through self-doubt, brighten a heavy day, or rekindle a fading sense of purpose. Yet the true beauty of a compliment lies not only in its immediate warmth but in its echo – how it alters the emotional landscape of the receiver, who, feeling seen and valued, becomes more inclined to uplift others in turn.

Thus, kindness radiates outward, like ripples on still water, touching lives far removed from the original moment. Over time, these small affirmations quietly reshape the culture of a community, weaving a fabric of empathy, encouragement, and connection.

In this way, a single sincere word can become a quiet revolution.

The Power and Philosophy of Saying No:

To say *no* is to reclaim the most precious gift you have: your time, your attention, your presence. In a world that often demands our constant acquiescence, the act of refusal is a radical assertion of self-sovereignty.

Saying *no* is not merely a rejection of an external offer or request – it is a profound affirmation of your inner boundaries and values. It is an expression of self-respect, a declaration that not everything deserves your consent or energy.

Yet, many struggle with this simple act, fearing disapproval, guilt, or the discomfort of conflict. But liberation begins when you recognise that every *no* creates space – space to breathe, to grow, to focus on what truly aligns with your essence.

Saying *no* may sometimes be uncomfortable or even humorous, but it always honours your truth. It is a vital act of preservation in a world hungry for our time and attention.

So, pause and reflect:

What have you recently said no to?

How much time and peace did you reclaim?

How did your spirit breathe freer without that burden?

In saying *no*, you do not close doors – you open yourself to a life lived intentionally, where your yes is not an obligation but a celebration.

Is It the Journey or the Destination? It's Neither:

Is it the journey or the destination? For years, I told myself it was neither – it's who you become along the way. Like lifting weights, the load doesn't get lighter; instead, you grow stronger. True self-worth doesn't come from the visible results, but from the discipline and commitment – the daily choice to show up and become.

Yet, there's a paradox that lingers in my mind: what if the journey isn't about becoming something new at all? What if it's about shedding the layers of who we were told to be – those expectations from school, university, work – the masks we wore to fit in, to succeed? Perhaps true growth lies in the act of unbecoming all that isn't authentically ours, revealing the self that was always there beneath it all.

In this light, life is not a quest to build ourselves up but a path of gentle peeling away, a return to our original essence. The destination isn't ahead; it's within – waiting quietly for us to come home.

You Are the Journey:

Do not carry life's experiences as a wound but treat them as a step to wisdom!

You've already achieved goals you said would make you happy, so why aren't you?

It is better to be unique than to be the best. Because, being the best makes you the number one and the focus is on being better than others, but being unique makes you the only one and not comparable to others.

> *"The unexamined life is not worth living."*
>
> – Socrates

Life isn't just about going through the motions. It's about pausing, reflecting, and questioning what really matters. When you take the time to understand your choices and purpose, you're not just living, you're truly alive. That's where meaning and fulfilment come from.

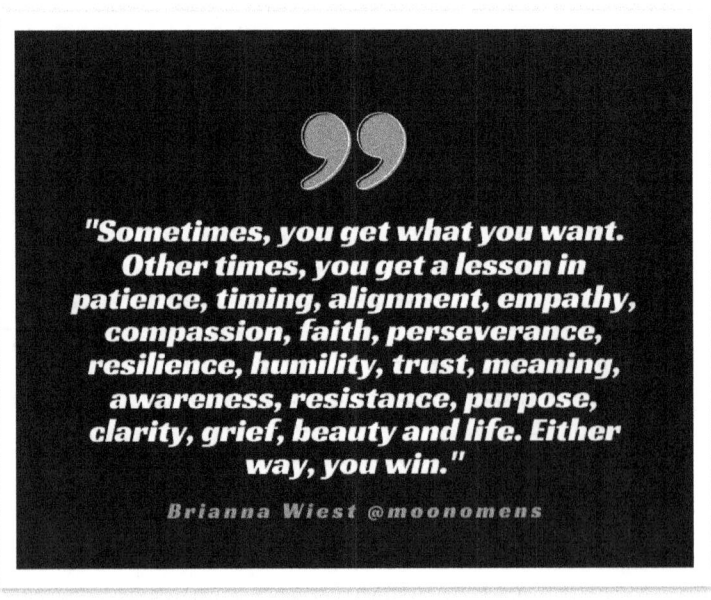

Know Who You Are Today:

Gratitude – Your Normal Day is Someone's Dream:

Articulating Your Emotions Is Easy:

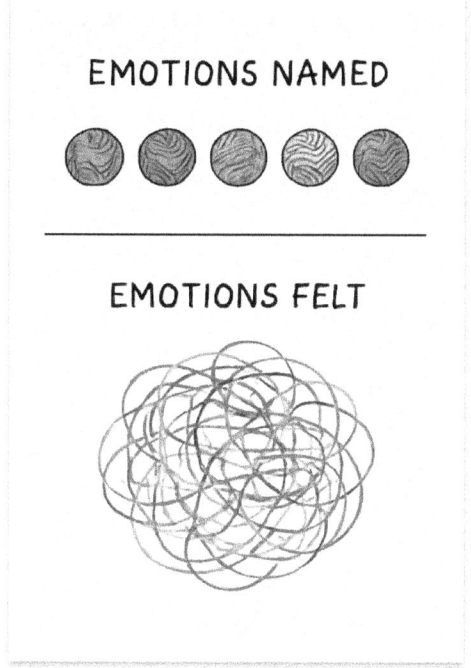

Managing Emotions and Thoughts:

To manage your emotions and thoughts, start by recognising a profound truth: experiences have no inherent meaning. They are like blank canvases, neither good nor bad, until your mind paints them with interpretation. It's not the events themselves, but the stories and emotions you attach to them that shape your inner world.

This awareness invites a deeper philosophical understanding: Every feeling you experience is a lens through which you interpret reality, consciously or unconsciously. When you feel an emotion rising within, pause and ask yourself:

"Out of all the emotions I could experience – anger, fear, joy, calmness, love, or even confusion – why have I chosen this one?"

This question calls you to mindfulness, reminding you that your inner state is a reflection of your chosen perspective. Later, in quiet reflection, ask again:

"How did this emotion serve me? Did it bring clarity, growth, or peace, or did it obscure my judgement and deepen suffering?"

This practice is vital. It encourages you to become a philosopher of your own mind, continuously examining and refining your emotional responses. Through this process, you release destructive emotions, disengage from unhelpful patterns, and cultivate a peaceful, intentional way of being.

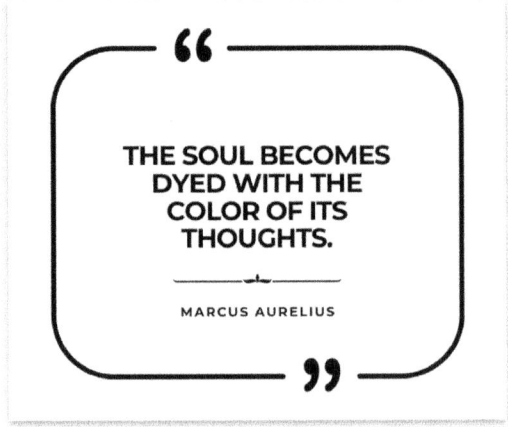

Authenticity / Being True to Yourself:

"I was ashamed of myself when I realised life was a costume party and I attended with my real face."

– Franz Kafka

In today's world, fake has become the new normal, so much so that authenticity feels unacceptable. This leads to authenticity being misunderstood… or trashed.

If you don't stand for the things you truly believe in, if you only say what others want to hear, if you "live an untrue life", then don't be surprised when you attract disingenuous people.

Living inauthentically is like looking at yourself in a hall of mirrors: you'll see reflections everywhere but never the true you.

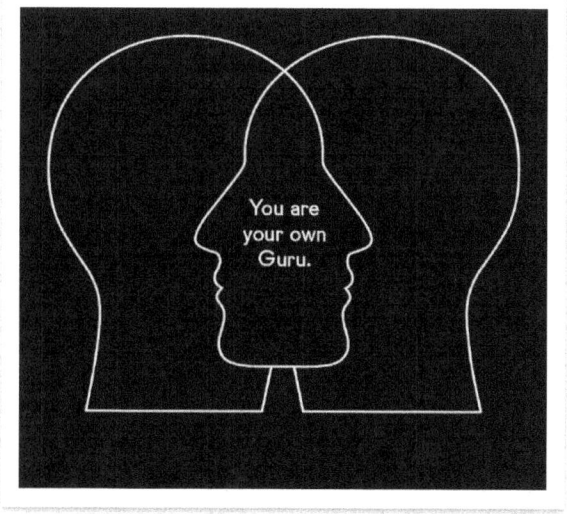

Fall in Love With Your Life:

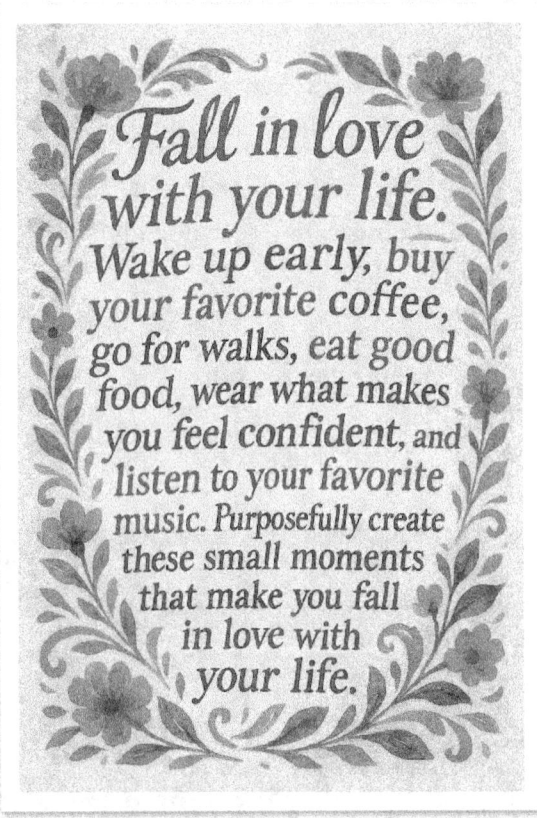

Reputation, Character & the Age of Applause:

In today's world, reputation is currency – followers, likes, and impressions are the new social capital. A well-curated image can open doors, win admiration, and build influence. Yet behind many polished profiles lie hollow foundations, with people more concerned about looking virtuous than being virtuous.

"It is not the man who has too little, but the man who craves more, that is poor."

– Seneca

Craving public approval has become a lifestyle. Every moment is filtered, every opinion tailored, every flaw concealed. Social media rewards the mask, not the face behind it. Stoicism reminds us: reputation is borrowed, but character is owned. The more you chase applause, the more you betray your inner compass.

"If you live in harmony with nature you will never be poor; if you live according to what others think, you will never be rich."

– Seneca

Many appear successful, confident, or wise, but when tested, they crumble. Why? They built their identity on perception, not principle. Stoicism calls us to a deeper foundation – one that doesn't need an audience. Character is forged in solitude. It's who you are when no one's watching, when there's nothing to post, and nothing to prove.

Reputation, Character & the Age of Applause – Part 2:

> *"Waste no more time arguing what a good man should be. Be one."*
>
> – Marcus Aurelius

The Stoic doesn't reject reputation – but he doesn't serve it either. He knows that praise is sweet but fleeting, and criticism is loud but often hollow. What matters is whether your life is aligned. When your actions reflect your values, when you do the right thing even when it costs you – then you walk with a rare kind of peace.

In a world obsessed with *appearing*, strive to *be*. Let the world misunderstand you if it must. You'll sleep better being unknown and real, than being admired and fake.

Reflection – Needs to Be Self-Reflective:

> **Even introspection and reflection can end up breeding negativity within us.**
>
> **This is why it's important to ensure the things we ponder are for our own benefit, and not for evaluating the faults of others to make ourselves feel superior.**

Becoming the Self You Are Meant to Be:

To truly step into your future self is to engage in a profound act of creation – an intentional rewriting of the narrative you hold about who you are and who you are becoming. The future self is not a distant ideal but a present reality waiting to be embodied here and now. Our identity shapes our experience; it is the lens through which the world is perceived and the foundation upon which habits are built. Thus, the transformation begins within: by altering the internal dialogue, by nurturing beliefs that reflect our highest potential, and by feeling deeply the emotions of the life we aspire to live.

To say "I am not ready" is to confine oneself to the past. Instead, affirm "I always rise to the occasion" – a declaration of faith in your inherent capacity to grow and adapt. Through consistent meditation, visualization, and gratitude, the subconscious mind is gently rewired, aligning thought and action with purpose.

The environment – physical, social, and mental – is the reflection of our inner state. To evolve, one must prune away the clutter, the toxic influences, and the dissonance that tether us to past versions of ourselves. Surrounding ourselves with expansive, supportive energy is not mere preference; it is a necessity for authentic becoming.

Ultimately, this journey is one of self-compassion and deliberate choice. You are already whole; you are already perfect in your striving.

"Your success is not a question of if, but when."

Step into your future self now, and watch as the life you envision unfolds with grace and inevitability.

We All Have Good and Bad Days:

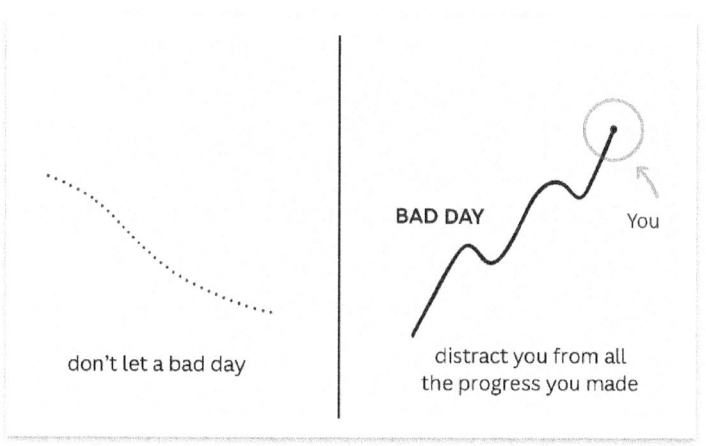

Self-Care Begins With Self-Truth:

Self-care is often misunderstood as a checklist – yoga, clean eating, eight hours of sleep, the gym, meditation. Each of these is undeniably beneficial, yet their true power lies not in the act itself, but in the *intention* behind it. You can stretch your body into perfect poses, fill your plate with nutrients, and sleep through the night – and still feel empty. Why? Because without aligned intention, even the most disciplined routine becomes another performance.

If you move your body to impress, eat to conform, sleep just to optimize, or meditate to feel superior, you may be improving your image – but not your soul. The real nourishment comes from *why* you do these things. Do you care for yourself because you deeply believe you are worth caring for? Or because you're chasing approval, validation, or escape?

Intention is the silent architect of peace. It is the unseen foundation of self-respect. When your actions arise from a place of love, not fear – from sincerity, not social pressure – then even the simplest act becomes sacred.

> *"It is not about what you do, but the energy you do it with."*

A single breath taken mindfully can heal more than hours of forced ritual.

True self-care is not aesthetic, it's internal. It is the quiet, courageous decision to honour your well-being because *you matter to yourself*, even when no one is watching. Peace isn't found in perfection, but in the purity of your intention.

The Root of Self-Respect:

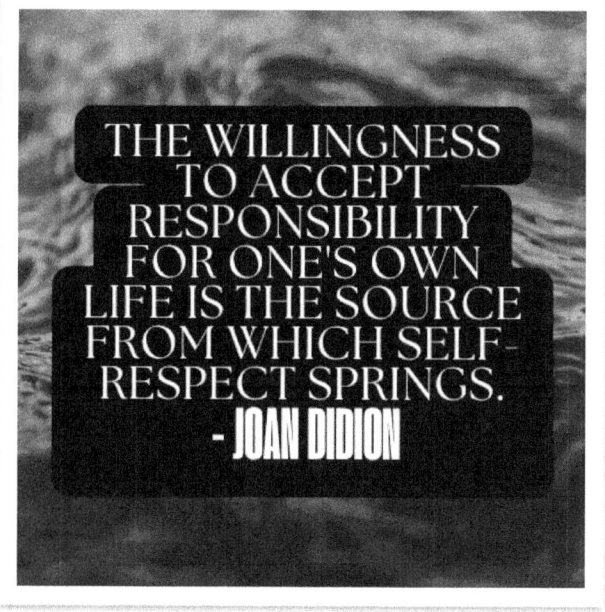

The Quiet Strength of Self-Sufficiency:

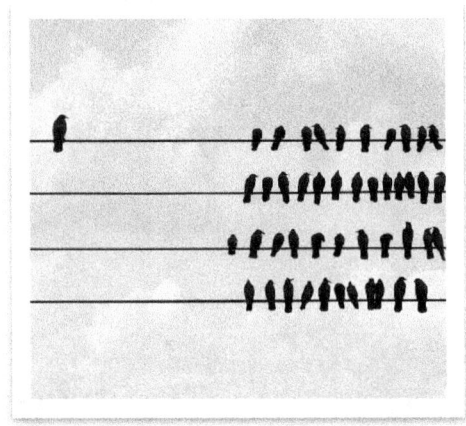

"Hyper-independence is a noble trait with the most unshakeable people needing nothing from anybody."

There's a quiet nobility in being able to stand on your own. However, hyper-independence often grows from past wounds – moments where relying on others led to disappointment or pain. So, some people learn to carry their own weight, to expect nothing, and to become their own safe haven.

From the outside, this looks like strength – and in many ways, it is. The most unshakeable people are those who've built inner stability so solid, they no longer seek approval, validation, or support to feel whole. They choose connection, but don't depend on it. This kind of self-sufficiency can be misunderstood, but at its core, it's not about coldness – it's about surviving, healing, and ultimately becoming free.

When you need nothing, you are untouchable.

Part II: Relationships, Influence & Community

Themes: Love, Connection, Communication, Boundaries

Protect the Family You Build – Always:

Never sit at a table where your spouse and children aren't welcome – not even if the table is one you came from, or one you helped build.

The people you choose to build a life with should never be made to feel like outsiders – not by family, not by friends, not by anyone else you allow into your world. If those closest to you cannot respect the ones you love most, then that space – no matter how familiar or comfortable – is not truly for you.

The family you create – your spouse, your children – is more than just a part of your life. They *are* your life. They are your home, your heart, and the legacy you leave behind.

Protect that family with everything you have. Stand up for them. Speak up for them. And never prioritise comfort, tradition, social circles, or loyalty to others above their well-being and dignity.

There may come a time when the family you came from, or the friends you've had for years, stop supporting your path – or simply don't align with the values you're raising your own family on.

In those moments, your responsibility is clear: **choose wisely.**
And the right choice will always be the people you committed to love, honour, and protect.

Because the truest test of character isn't who you are when it's easy – it's who you are when you're asked to choose.

The Journey of Connection:

> Time decides who you meet in life.
>
> Your heart decides who you want in your life.
>
> Your behavior decides who stays in your life.

The Sacred Space of Genuine Care:

To truly care for someone is to move beyond the surface question, "How are you?" It is easy to offer these words as a polite gesture, but genuine care demands we dive deeper – into the spaces where vulnerability lives, where unspoken struggles quietly persist. Depth in conversation is not merely about exchanging words; it is about creating a sacred space where empathy can breathe.

When we ask how someone is really doing, we are inviting them to step out from behind their masks, to share the hidden contours of their experience. This requires patience, presence, and a willingness to listen without judgement or hurry. True empathy is not about offering solutions or rushing to fix, but about holding the complexity of another's feelings with compassion.

Until the Lesson Is Learned:

Both Reshma and I grew up in Hindu homes where certain beliefs were repeatedly mentioned or talked about. One of those beliefs is that *"you will keep meeting the same person in different bodies until you learn the lesson."*

While modern in phrasing, it reflects a profound truth: life is a classroom, and relationships are among its most rigorous teachers. According to the doctrine of *samsara* – the cycle of birth, death, and rebirth – we are not born into random circumstances. We are bound by *karma*, the spiritual law of cause and effect, which carries unresolved energies, desires, and lessons from life to life.

In this view, the people who enter our lives are not accidents, but echoes – mirrors of unresolved parts of ourselves, returning again and again until we see what they have come to reveal. The "same person" is not a literal recurrence, but a recurring pattern – of betrayal, of love, of abandonment, of control – playing out through new faces and fresh dynamics. These souls are cast in different roles, but the lesson remains unchanged.

Hinduism teaches that liberation (*moksha*) comes through awareness rather than avoidance. We are meant to confront these patterns consciously, to transform reaction into realisation. Only when we no longer resist, when we understand the root of our entanglement – be it ego, attachment, fear, or pride – does the cycle break. The "person" vanishes, not because they stop appearing, but because the inner need for that experience dissolves.

Thus, the universe is not punishing us, but guiding us – with infinite patience – toward clarity. Until we learn the lesson, life will hand us the same script in different costumes. But when we finally see the pattern and embrace the growth it demands, we no longer meet the same person. We meet ourselves, and find that we've changed. And that, perhaps, was the lesson all along.

Don't Let the Warmth Fade Away:

Don't leave your coffee sitting too long...

and then act surprised when it turns cold.

(I'm not talking about coffee.)

Don't Underestimate Your Sphere of Influence:

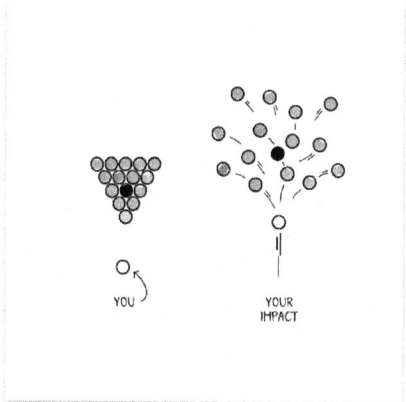

If someone shares an achievement, go out of your way to say "well done" If you like someone's outfit or work, make sure you give them a compliment.

A few kind words can change someone's day. With all the negative comparisons and bullying online, we could use more kindness.

Don't underestimate the power of a few kind words.

There are people who carry you with them, even in ways you may never see.

Read that again.

There are people that carry you with them.

How powerful is that?

Someone, somewhere, is braver or happier because of a moment they shared with you. They saw something in you that cracked open a space within them. There is a person who still saves your words in their subconscious, tucking them away like a note pressed between pages. You have been someone's inspiration... unseen but present, taking in the way you rise and fall and rise again. They have watched you persist, and because of that, they believe that they can too.

And whether or not you realise it, your presence has left something lasting

"The world needs more people like you."

Reclaiming Power – Boundaries, Truth, and the Narcissist's Illusion:

"A narcissist gets angry with you when you find out the truth about them."

Having moved through the boardrooms of some of the world's largest companies and witnessed the subtle power plays among school parents, I've come to a profound realisation about human nature: narcissists do not merely resist truth – they rage against it. This anger is not just defensiveness; it is a fragile ego's desperate attempt to preserve its carefully constructed illusion.

To hold such people accountable is to engage in a quiet but radical act of self-respect. It begins with setting clear boundaries and intentions, not as weapons but as declarations of one's worth. And when those boundaries are violated, the wisest response is often not confrontation, but deliberate withdrawal – a refusal to feed the cycle of disrespect.

The true challenge lies not in their actions, but in our reactions. Narcissistic manipulation, especially gaslighting, seeks to invert reality, making us question our own perceptions and doubt our rightful indignation. This distortion is a subtle poison, eroding the foundation of self-trust.

Yet, through the lens of experience – whether in corporate power corridors or social microcosms – I have learned that strength is found in steadfastness to one's truth. To recognise manipulation for what it is, to hold firm without surrendering to chaos, is to reclaim our power. In this, we find not only survival but liberation – a quiet triumph over the destructive dance of control and deception.

"They Know What They Did" – A Meditation on Silent Boundaries:

When asked why one severs ties without words, the answer:

"They know what they did," echoes with more weight than mere dismissal.

It is not silence out of spite, but silence as a final judgement – a quiet verdict rendered after the court of patience has long recessed.

In a world where noise often substitutes for meaning, silence becomes sacred. It is in most cases not the coward's retreat; it is the philosopher's shield.

To walk away without explanation is to refuse further distortion, to deny the guilty the comfort of feigned ignorance. It is to recognise that the act was not done in darkness – it was done in full view of conscience. And so, the silence is not absence, but presence – the presence of consequence.

This is not about punishment, but about peace. A soul that has wrestled with betrayal, disappointment, or repeated harm eventually learns that not all wounds must be narrated to be healed. Not all departures must be announced. Some doors are closed with a whisper – not because the pain is small, but because the self-respect is great.

The silent cut-off, then, is not cruelty. It is clarity. And those who truly wonder why the silence came, perhaps were not listening when the noise still begged for understanding.

First Impressions – Be Cautious:

Be Wary of First Impressions

The first impression you encounter sticks in your mind, setting unrealistic expectations. Before making decisions, always do your own research. Challenge your own assumptions.

Ask yourself: Am I considering all options or just the first one I saw?

Telling People That Their "Baby's Ugly":

Never tell someone their "baby is ugly" – whether that baby is an idea, a new venture, or a personal passion project.

People rarely want the unvarnished truth. More often, what they're really asking is, *"Please confirm that I'm not delusional for loving this thing I poured my soul into."*

What we call feedback is usually a polite ritual – a socially acceptable way to fish for validation without seeming needy.

Behind every pitch, manuscript, or start-up is someone's late nights, fragile hopes, and internal pep talks. So, yes – be honest, but also be kind. Because while honesty is a virtue, bluntness is just laziness dressed up as virtue.

And listen – this book is *my* baby. I've nurtured it, stressed over it, lost sleep over it, and yes, I think it's kind of adorable. So if you're tempted to tell me it has weird ears or a big nose... please remember: no one wants to hear their baby's ugly. Just lie to me gently, or at least cushion the blow with a bottle of wine.

The Quiet Power of Discretion:

There is profound wisdom in the art of discretion – an ancient strategy that teaches us the power of silence and subtlety in a world that often values noise and spectacle. To *buy land in secret* and *build the house quietly* is to nurture one's dreams away from the distractions of judgement, envy, and misunderstanding. It is in these hidden moments that vision takes root and strength gathers unseen. When the *housewarming party* finally arrives, when the *marriage* is celebrated publicly, the foundation has long been laid – solid, unwavering, and unshaken by external voices.

Discretion guards the sacred space between intention and action. Like a game of chess, life demands we move with purpose and patience. The greatest players do not reveal their strategies or boast of their plans. They do not speak until the final move – the moment of *checkmate* – when victory is undeniable and the world can no longer deny their truth.

To broadcast your vision prematurely is to invite division, distraction, and doubt. Let the haters see only the reality you have built, not the fragile hopes or grand designs still unfolding in the quiet. Your power lies in acting, not speaking; in building silently, not announcing; in achieving steadily, not shouting. Your achievements – when they come – are your true checkmate, the final word that needs no defence or explanation.

In this way, discretion is not secrecy born of fear, but a strategic choice of strength, humility, and wisdom. It is the silent dance of progress, the quiet assertion of purpose, and the calm confidence that true success requires no fanfare – only the undeniable proof of what has been quietly accomplished.

Setting Boundaries – The Price of Access:

Setting boundaries is not cruelty – it is clarity.

It is the quiet, courageous act of deciding that your peace, your energy, and your self-respect are worth protecting. Never forget: *you* set the price of access to you. That price is called a boundary, and you are allowed – no, *empowered* – to change it as you grow.

When someone responds to your boundary with resistance, remember: their discomfort is not your responsibility, but their disrespect is not your burden to carry.

You can grieve someone's absence and still refuse to lower your standards for the sake of keeping them. Because every time you tolerate what harms you, you silently declare it acceptable. And you are not here to validate disrespect – you are here to live in truth, even if that truth requires walking alone.

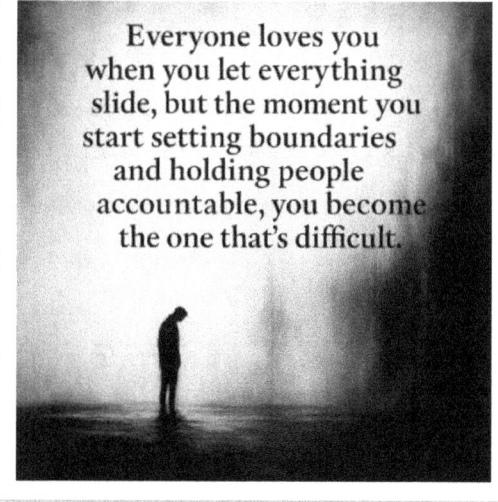

Knowing Where You Stand With People:

"Do people love yourself for who you are or for what you do?"

This is uncomfortable to consider.

People loving us for who we are feels more real, genuine, caring, empathetic and robust. It feels like it's less fickle and more difficult to lose.

On the other hand, people loving us for what we do feels transactional and transient. The love we receive becomes contingent on what achievements and successes we can offer in return.

And the obvious fear is that if a point came where we no longer had anything to offer in return, would our love be taken away?

So here's an even more uncomfortable question...

"Do you love yourself for who you are or for what you do?"

This highlights our hypocrisy.

You see, we want the world to love us for who we are. A balanced, caring view of our true value, independent of our accomplishments.

Meanwhile, our own self-love is largely determined by what we do.

If we fall short, even though we know we tried our best, we still castigate ourselves for being insufficient, unworthy creatures.

So we want the world to show up for us in a way that we are often not prepared to show up for ourselves.

You deserve more than this. Demand it of yourself.

Having People That Challenge Your Perspective:

> People who introduce
> you to new ways
> of thinking and new
> ways of seeing life
> are so important.

The Power of Inverse Charisma:

"There is a great man who makes every man feel small. But the real great man is the man who makes every man feel great."

Olivia Fox Cabane shares this leadership lesson from the Victorian era England. Two men, Benjamin Disraeli and William Gladstone, were competing for the position of the prime minister of the United Kingdom. Both were brilliant, clever, witty, and had what it took to win the election. What made the difference, however, was summed up by a woman who had dinner with both Disraeli and Gladstone a week before the election. When a journalist asked her what her impression of the two men was, she responded: "When I left the dining room after sitting next to Gladstone, I thought he was the cleverest man in England. But when I sat next to Disraeli, I left feeling that I was the cleverest woman."

Isn't that interesting? Disraeli had mastered the art of making other people see their own worth, feel better, respected, and important. Disraeli had what psychologist Adam Grant calls, inverse charisma. Charisma is when someone is gifted at drawing other people to themselves. We think of charisma as a charm, a power to attract. Inverse charisma is the ability to see and bring out the best in others.

Rather than trying to make yourself seem interesting, focus on making the other people feel interesting. Listen to the message, ask questions, don't talk over people, be fully engaged in the conversation – you will embolden the speaker and they will rise in their eyes but also yours.

> **To inspire people, don't show them your super powers. Show them theirs.**

The Beauty Within – Instilling Pride in Our Children:

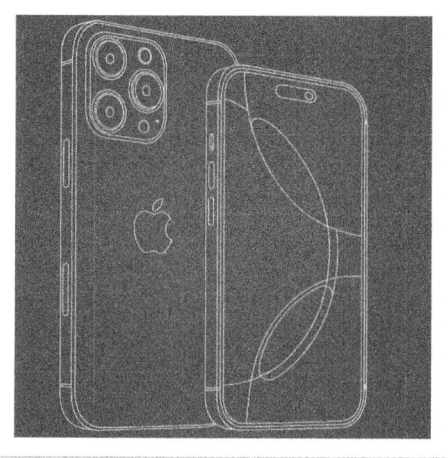

This is something I feel deeply about. In a world where speed often matters more than quality and cutting corners is common, Steve Jobs teaches us that true pride comes from caring about the details, even the ones no one notices.

Jobs's commitment to excellence offers an important lesson for raising exceptional children.

As a teenager, he helped his father build a fence. When Jobs wondered why they needed to paint the back of the fence – a part no one would see – his father said, "You've got to make the back of the fence, that nobody will see, just as good as the front." This lesson taught Jobs that true quality comes from caring about every detail, even the unseen ones.

This belief shaped his work at Apple. Jobs made sure that even the parts of products like the iPhone, hidden from users, were carefully designed. He thought this attention to detail reflected the integrity of the product and of its creators.

By teaching these values, we can help our children grow into people who care about excellence and integrity, laying the foundation for great character and achievements.

Charity Dressed Up as Dignity:

There is a subtle grace in the way true kindness is offered – not as pity, but as respect. I once read a simple story that revealed this truth beautifully:

"My father used to buy simple goods from poor people at high prices, even though he did not need them. Sometimes he even used to pay extra for them.

Concerned, I asked why he would do such a thing.

He replied, "It is charity wrapped in dignity, my child."

In this answer lies a profound lesson: true charity is not about giving from a place of superiority, but about honouring the humanity of others. To offer help disguised as respect preserves the recipient's pride and sense of worth. It recognises that dignity is as vital a currency as money itself.

When charity is given without dignity, it can diminish both giver and receiver. But when wrapped in respect, it becomes an exchange of humanity – one that uplifts rather than lowers, that connects rather than divides.

This kind of charity teaches us that kindness need not echo as a handout, but can sing softly as a shared moment of grace.

You Would be Amazed at How Others See You:

We often underestimate our own value and impact because we tend to be overly critical or focused on our flaws.

When others look at us, they usually see qualities, strengths, and positive traits that we might not notice or fully appreciate ourselves.

If you could see yourself through the eyes of people who care about you or respect you, you'd likely be surprised – and even amazed – by how much good there is in you. It's a reminder to be kinder to yourself and recognise your worth, even when self-doubt creeps in.

Burning Bridges – There Is No Coming Back:

> Once I'm detached, that's it. You will never get the same version of me. Ever.

Siblings – A Complex Journey of Love and Growth:

A sibling is a mirror, a rival, a companion, a witness.

From the earliest days, we're bound together by the gravity of our shared world: our parents, our home, the simple joys of childhood. We play in the garden together, hours of board games such as Monopoly, stay up late in our bunk beds, and argue every day – each moment carving out a bond that lasts. It's a bond formed by the ordinary, by being each other's first "other."

But as time moves on, life pulls us in different directions. Ambitions (for example, university) take us away, priorities change, and new relationships take shape. The old family home becomes a memory, and the bond we once took for granted starts to evolve into something new.

Yet, as my father always said, a brother, a sister – they're for life. No matter what happens. This truth runs deeper than a simple phrase. The connection we share, no matter how tested, is permanent. It requires care, not out of obligation, but because few can say they knew us before life changed us – and even fewer will truly know us at the end.

To keep a sibling relationship strong is to accept its paradox: unconditional love mixed with inevitable change. It's remembering that, no matter what path we take, we always share that beginning. And sometimes, in those quiet moments, that's enough – knowing that always, under any circumstance, you are always there for each other.

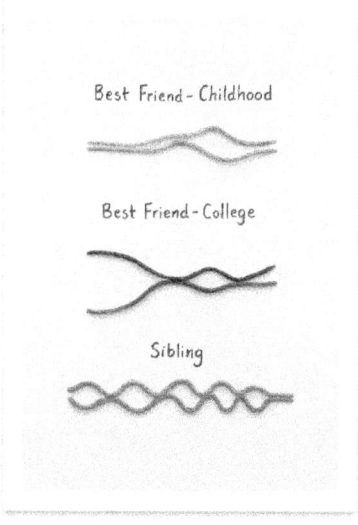

Energy in Relationships:

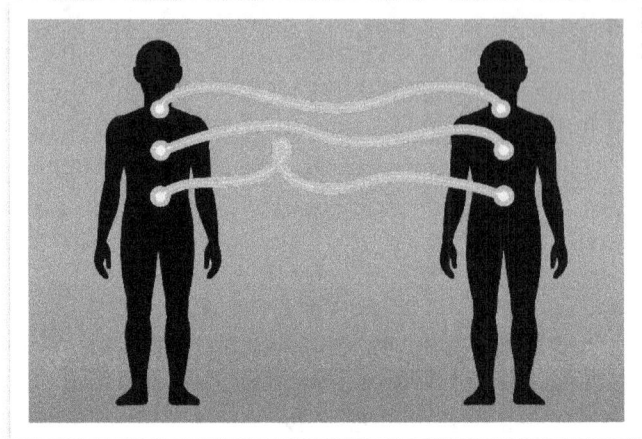

In relationships, the way we see others deeply impacts how we interact with them.

What if, instead of seeing people through labels – friend, family, co-worker – we viewed them as energy?

When you recognise people as energy sources, you become more aware of how their presence affects you. Some uplift and energise you, while others drain you. This awareness helps you protect your own energy and invest it wisely in relationships that nurture you.

Additionally, while people might envy your success, they often overlook the struggle it took to get there. Success is celebrated, but the hard work behind it rarely is. True supporters don't just admire your achievements – they respect the effort and challenges you faced to reach them.

Ultimately, the energy you share and receive in relationships is what defines their depth and value. Choose wisely who you invest your time and energy in, and focus on those who truly support you, both in your victories and your struggles.

"All You Need Is Love" by John Lennon – It's a choice to Prioritise Family:

John Lennon's decision to step away from his music career to focus on raising his son Sean stands as a profound testament to the power of re-evaluating one's priorities. In the mid-1970s, Lennon took a five-year hiatus from the music industry, embracing the role of a devoted house-husband.

He dedicated himself to daily routines like preparing meals and spending quality time with Sean, emphasising the significance of being present during his son's formative years.

This shift was deeply influenced by Lennon's own experiences of childhood abandonment, and the emotional revelations he encountered during primal therapy sessions with Dr. Arthur Janov. The therapy unearthed long-suppressed traumas, leading Lennon to confront the pain of his early years and inspiring him to break the cycle by being an actively involved father.

Lennon's journey underscores the idea that even amidst fame and demanding careers, prioritising family and personal healing can lead to profound fulfilment.

His story serves as a compelling reminder that reassessing our priorities can lead to transformative life choices, emphasising that it's never too late to focus on what truly matters.

Love as a Mirror:

Love is often spoken of as a feeling we give to another, but perhaps its deepest truth is more inward:

> *"You don't love the other people; you love the person you are and the person you are becoming when you are with that person."*

This suggests that love is as much about self-discovery as it is about connection. In the presence of someone else, we see ourselves reflected – not just as we are, but as we could be. Love becomes a mirror, showing us the potential, the courage, the tenderness that may have been hidden or dormant.

To love another is to embrace the transformation they inspire within us, the unfolding of a fuller self that is braver, softer, more alive. It is not possession or fixation on who they are, but a gratitude for who we become because of their presence. And in this, love transcends the simple act of being with someone – it becomes a sacred journey inward, a dance between two souls that awakens the best parts of each.

Love, then, is less about the other and more about becoming – becoming whole, becoming seen, becoming free.

We Say "Unconditional Love" – But What Do We Mean?:

We often talk about unconditional love, especially for our children. We say it's natural, something we give freely. But if we really look at how we show love, a different picture emerges: how often do we express love when there's nothing to praise?

We cheer for good grades, celebrate awards, and light up when they succeed, but go quiet when they don't. Without meaning to, we start teaching that love must be earned.

When did this shift happen? Maybe love was never truly unconditional. Maybe pressure from society, schools, work, or even our own upbringing shaped the way we love today. Maybe we're repeating what we were taught.

This matters. Conditional love tells children they are only worthy when they succeed. It turns love into something fragile – something they have to chase. That belief follows them into friendships, families, and future relationships. Many grow up feeling valued only for what they did, not who they were.

Unconditional love doesn't mean we ignore problems or lower standards. It means we stand by someone even when they fall. It says: *I love you when you fail. I love you when you feel lost. I love you because you're you – not because you did something right.*

We need to check ourselves. It's not just about *feeling* unconditional love – it's about *showing* it in everyday, quiet moments: when they come home with a bad grade, when they lose, when they disappoint us.

That's the world we should be creating.

The Most Important Decision in Life:

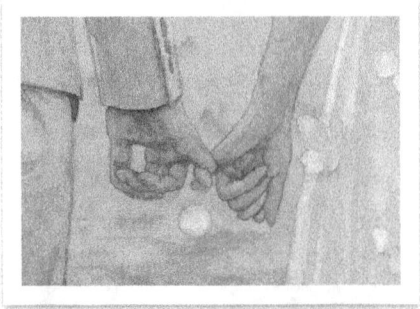

"You don't love someone for their looks, or their clothes, or for their fancy car, but because they sing a song only you can hear."

– Oscar Wilde

I'm proud to say Reshma and I have been married for nearly 30 years and together for over 40. It's the cornerstone of everything I am and drives my life.

Marrying the right person matters more than meeting societal milestones. Having kids with the right partner is far more important than just becoming a parent. This decision shapes:

Emotional and Mental Well-Being: A supportive, loving partner provides strength, stability, and comfort, while the wrong one can bring stress, depression, and emotional turmoil.

Life Trajectory and Personal Growth: The right person encourages growth, aligns with your values, and supports your goals.

Long-Term Companionship: Choosing the right partner means building a lasting friendship, sharing memories, and weathering life's ups and downs.

Family and Parenting: If you have children, a co-parent's values, stability, religion, and parenting style deeply influence your children's well-being.

Financial Stability: Couples should openly discuss finances, as Ramit Sethi encourages in *How to Live a Rich Life*.

Social Impact: Your spouse influences your social circle and reputation, and we're fortunate to share similar values with many of our friends.

The Invisible Thread Between Two Hearts:

A true partner is one who believes in your dreams even when you doubt them yourself. Like the friend who stays up late listening as you plan your future, or the person who cheers the loudest when you take a risk. They inspire you to grow into your best self, not by demanding change, but by walking beside you through life's challenges.

They don't just admire your successes – they are grateful for the person you are today, imperfections and all. Maybe it's the quiet support during your struggles or the small acts of kindness when no one is watching. Most importantly, your souls meet – a connection beyond words, beyond logic. You feel it in a glance, a touch, or the simple comfort of being understood.

Choosing a partner is not about titles or achievements. It's not about marrying a doctor, a lawyer, or someone with a fancy degree from Harvard or Oxford. Nor is it about surface things like looks or charm. And it's certainly not about marrying someone because of their potential – that hope that they'll "grow into" a better person.

> *"The more you can explain it based on specific characteristics it's not likely to work in the long run. There has to be a connection at a deeper level."*

Kafka's Beautiful Letters to a Girl:

At 40, Franz Kafka, who never married and had no children, walked through the park in Berlin when he met a girl who was crying because she had lost her favourite doll.

She and Kafka searched for the doll unsuccessfully. Kafka told her to meet him there the next day and they would come back to look for her.

The next day, when they had not yet found the doll, Kafka gave the girl a letter "written" by the doll saying "please don't cry. I took a trip to see the world. I will write to you about my adventures."

Thus began a story which continued until the end of Kafka's life.

During their meetings, Kafka read the letters of the doll carefully written with adventures and conversations that the girl found adorable. Finally, Kafka brought back the doll (he had bought one) that had returned to Berlin.

"It doesn't look like my doll at all," said the girl.

Kafka handed her another letter in which the doll wrote: "my travels have changed me." the little girl hugged the new doll and brought the doll with her to her happy home.

A year later, Kafka died.

Many years later, the now-adult girl found a letter inside the doll. In the tiny letter signed by Kafka, it was written:

"Everything you love will probably be lost, but in the end, love will return in another way."

The Truest Form of Love:

Richard Feynman, Nobel laureate in Physics, wrote the most moving letter to his late wife Arline in 1946, after her death. Described as one of the most beautiful expressions of true love, it remained sealed in an envelope marked *"To Arline Feynman. I love you, Richard"* and was discovered after his death. The letter was never sent, because as Feynman heartbreakingly noted, *"You can't."*

In this letter, Feynman's love for Arline is clear, not in grand gestures, but in simple, aching truth. "I adore you, my darling." His love persists beyond her death, as he writes, *"I find it hard to understand what it means to love you after you are dead – but I still want to comfort and take care of you."* His love isn't an idealised memory; it's a living, breathing love, grounded in shared moments.

Feynman's pain is profoundly human, expressed without melodrama. He confesses his loneliness, saying:

> *"I want to tell you I love you. I want to love you. I always will. I want to have problems to discuss with you – I want to do little projects with you."*

Perhaps the most heartbreaking line is: *"You, dead, are so much better than anyone else alive."* True love isn't the absence of grief, but the presence of someone in your heart so deeply that not even death can dim their light. Feynman's letter shows us that love doesn't end – it evolves, waits, and speaks, even in silence.

The Quiet Power of Labels – Yourself and Your Kids:

Be careful how you label yourself. Be even more careful how you label your children.

Words are not just sounds – they are seeds. What we speak over ourselves and others takes root in the mind, shaping how we see the world and how the world sees us. A label may seem small, even harmless, but it can quietly anchor itself in identity and grow into belief.

Labelling theory teaches us that identity is not fixed – it is formed. A child called "shy" may become withdrawn. A student told they are "not academic" may stop trying. A person labelled "trouble" may begin to live it, not because it is true, but because it has been spoken as truth. As the philosopher Epictetus said:

> *"It's not events that disturb us, but our interpretation of them."*

So too with identity – it is not who we are that defines us, but how we are told to see ourselves. A label is not just a description; it is a prescription. It suggests a path, narrows possibility, and can quietly turn into a self-fulfilling prophecy.

And often, it is not what the child is, but how the adult sees them that becomes the lens through which they learn to see themselves.

Instead of saying, *"You're lazy,"* say, *"You're still learning how to focus."*
Instead of *"You're bad at this,"* say, *"You haven't mastered it yet."*

The words we choose are brushstrokes on the canvas of identity. And every child is a masterpiece in the making.

The Heartbreak of a Child is When a Parent Does Not Really Know Them:

> "My greatest pain is that you never got to know me and never wanted to know me."
>
> — **Forough Farrokhzad**, from a letter to her father written c. January 1957

Your Parents' Voice:

"You never know how precious your Father's voice is until you no longer hear it."

In the quiet spaces left behind, we come to understand that a voice is more than sound – it's a presence, a compass, a tether to our earliest sense of safety. It's the echo of guidance, love, and sometimes, silent strength.

Only when that voice fades do we realise how deeply it shaped the rhythms of our days and the quiet corners of our hearts.

Absence teaches us the fragile treasure of connection, reminding us that some gifts are only fully seen in their loss.

Having Children Is Our Second act – First Act Was Ourselves:

There is no right answer for when to have children, it comes down to personal maturity, depth of relationship and how fulfilled you are as people.

In the tapestry of our lives, we chose to thread the needle of parenthood not in haste, but with deliberate grace. We first sought to understand the world and ourselves – establishing careers and breaking glass ceilings, taking a round-the-world trip, and embracing the myriad experiences life offered.

Only when our hearts and minds were ready did we welcome children into our journey. And this path, though divergent from the conventional, bestowed upon us profound insights. Our emotional maturity, honed through years of life's trials and triumphs, became the bedrock of our parenting.

Financial stability, the benefits of both Reshma and I having established careers, allowed us to invest our time, and provide a secure environment for our family. The quote from CS Lewis is a powerful reminder of what the priority should be when you choose to become parents.

> *"Children are not a distraction from more important work. They are the most important work."*
>
> – C.S. Lewis

To conclude, our decision to have children when we felt truly prepared has been the most rewarding choice of our lives. It allowed us to offer our children not just life, but a life enriched with our presence, wisdom, and stability.

Parenting in a New Era:

"Parenting is where you spend your life teaching the people you can't live without... To live without you..."

This is one of the hardest quotes to read, it's hard-hitting in its simplicity.

It's not that easy, especially when our own role models were often our parents, and in many cases they were simply too busy surviving.

Hopefully, it's different for our generation. We're better educated, and have the capacity to make conscious parenting decisions. The challenge though is that in many cases we lack the "broader village" to help raise our kids.

So, one day in the future, when your child sits across from someone and describes what it was like to be raised by you...

Make sure it's a story worth telling.

Letting Children Become:

The relationship between parent and child is often misunderstood – not as a rigid form of control, but as a quiet structure meant to protect growth. A child asks, *"Why do you keep stopping me from doing things?"* And the parent replies, *"Why do cars have brakes?"* The child answers, *"To slow you down."* But the deeper truth emerges: *"No, it's to allow you to go faster. Without brakes, you'd have to move cautiously, afraid to crash."*

This exchange speaks to the essence of loving guidance. Limits are not walls; they are tools that make freedom possible. A child who understands boundaries can move through life more boldly, knowing there is safety in structure. But guidance must never be confused with projection. Too often, parents carry invisible burdens – unfulfilled dreams, fears, or rigid ideals – and place them on the shoulders of their children. And when children don't match those inherited expectations, they are punished not for who they are, but for who they are not.

The highest form of parenting is not control, but presence – seeing the child not as a reflection of the parent's ego, but as their own becoming. Boundaries with love, not pressure. Guidance with empathy, not projection. Because the point of brakes is not to slow the journey – it's to make the full journey possible.

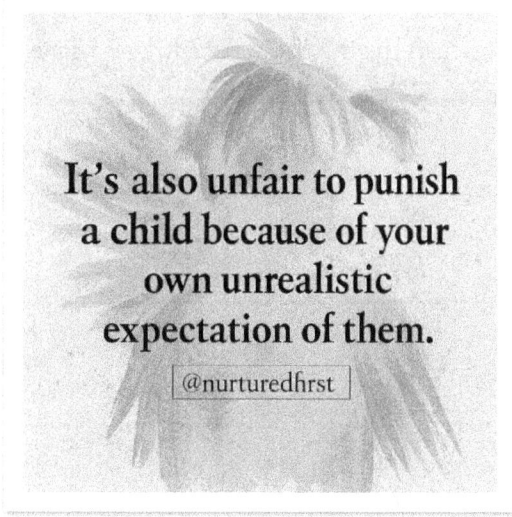

Reflections on Children – Keeping Them Grounded:

What I've always known, but now feel more deeply, is the quiet power of taking our children back to where Reshma and I came from – to the homes and streets of our own childhoods.

Time with grandparents and our siblings has always mattered, especially when they were young. But there's something deeper when they walk the same spaces we once did, free from the noise of modern distractions. It roots them. It reminds them – and us – of what truly shapes character: simplicity, humility, connection.

There is something sacred in watching them learn from their elders. Not through instruction, but through presence. In these moments, virtue is not taught; it is absorbed.

A meaningful life is often invisible in the moment. It's made of the things our older selves would one day wish we'd cherished more while we still had the gift of youth. We forget how brief even a long life is. And yet, the wisdom is already within us – calling softly in the direction of truth, urging us to follow where our hearts already point.

The Home You Raise Your Children in Becomes a Part of Their DNA:

Do Not Ask Your Kids to Chase Extraordinary Lives:

Do not ask your children to chase extraordinary lives, as if meaning only exists on the peaks. The world will already whisper that they must be more, do more, prove more. But we, as their parents, have a quieter truth to offer: that wonder does not live in grand achievements – it breathes in the ordinary.

Teach them to notice the world with open eyes. To marvel at the sun cutting through morning mist, to find reverence in the rhythm of rain, to feel the holiness in a simple shared meal. Show them how to love fully, to grieve deeply, to sit with silence without fear. Let them taste the fullness of life in things most people rush past.

For a child who can see the sacred in the ordinary will never be poor in spirit. And a life lived with that awareness becomes extraordinary without ever needing to strive. We do not need to push our children toward greatness. We need to teach them to pay attention – because when they do, greatness finds them.

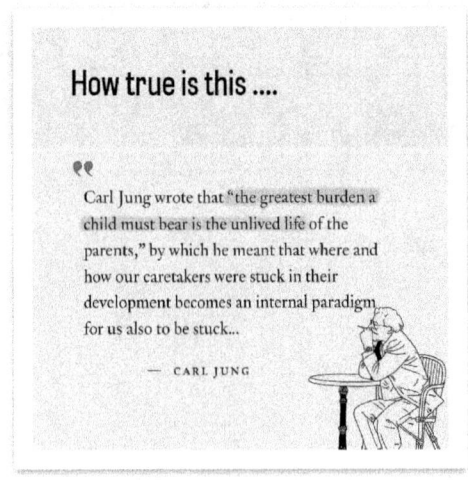

Parenting Beyond Dependence:

Parenting is not just raising a child, it's becoming the adult you once needed.

It means showing up with patience when no one did, offering love where there was absence, and teaching strength where you felt weak. You train them not to need you forever, but to want you by their side – a presence they cherish, not a crutch they depend on.

To guide a child is to heal your own past wounds. In this, we break cycles – not just for them, but for ourselves. Be the adult you needed, and watch a new world grow.

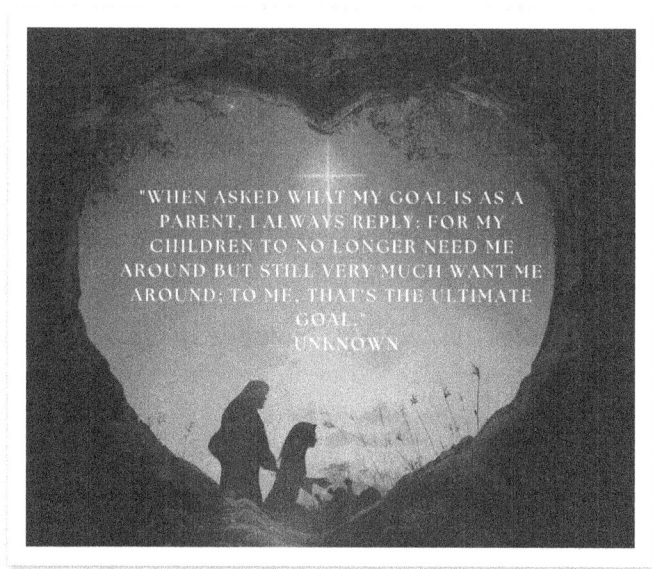

Re-incarnation or Heaven – Our Children Are Our Afterlife:

Throughout cosmic time, the quest for immortality has often been sought through spiritual beliefs in an afterlife. In my Hindu home, reincarnation and karma were frequent topics. However, Richard Dawkins, the British evolutionary biologist, offers a biological reframing: the afterlife isn't a disembodied soul, but the persistence of one's genetic code through generations. In *The Selfish Gene*, Dawkins writes:

> *"We are survival machines – robot vehicles blindly programmed to preserve the selfish molecules known as genes."*

What truly survives us is not our self, but our DNA carried by our children. This shifts the focus from ego to genes, the fundamental units of biological information. Our legacy is encoded not only in memories or monuments but in the molecules that make us.

Emotional wounds and fears can echo across generations, but so can healing and strength. We are not just passive transmitters of DNA but active editors of our lineage. By addressing our inner demons, we shift the very code our children inherit.

Dawkins's idea of the "second life" is not just genetic replication, but a recalibration – an emotional and biological echo in the evolution of life. As he says, "Genes are the immortals, or at least long-term survivors." Our children carry this immortality, becoming living monuments to both our existence and transformation.

To have children is to partake in the eternal cycle. To change ourselves is to shape that cycle.

Peace Over Pressure – Parenting Beyond Outcomes:

Having children means watching them face challenges, like exam stress, and learning to navigate it alongside them. Reshma and I have been clear: we are not outcome-driven. Exams are simply part of the journey, not the destination.

Stress often comes when we fixate on a specific result and lose sight of the present moment. When the joy of learning and growing fades beneath the weight of expectation, stress inevitably follows.

As Epictetus wisely said:

"Make the best use of what is in your power, and take the rest as it happens."

This reminds us that peace depends not on external outcomes – things often beyond our control – but on how we choose to respond to them. When we cling tightly to results, we invite frustration. But when we find meaning in the effort itself – in showing up, learning, and growing – we free ourselves from that burden.

Marcus Aurelius captured this beautifully:

"You have power over your mind – not outside events. Realise this, and you will find strength."

For me, and for Reshma, embracing what we can control – our mindset, our support, our presence – is the key to facing stress with calm. The rest, we try to accept with grace.

The Power of Connecting Beyond the Surface:

Lately I've realised… everyone looks like they're actually doing okay until you sit them down and have a real and honest conversation with them.

Then it hits you…we're part of a generation that is quietly struggling behind smiles and filtered pictures…

Making someone feel that they've been heard is so powerful! Don't underestimate "your bank" on which to pull from. How you deal with anything:

Our busy lives and difficulties in life present us with an opportunity to turn inward and to invoke our own inner resources. The trials we endure can and should introduce us to our strengths. Prudent people look beyond the incident itself and seek to form the habit of putting it to good use. On the occasion of an accidental event, don't just react in a haphazard fashion: remember to turn inward and ask what resources you have for dealing with it. Dig deeply.

> *"You possess strengths you might not realise you have. Find the right one. Use it."*
>
> – Epictetus

The quietest and most peaceful place is within your own soul. In a world full of noise and endless distractions, meditation and flow offers a retreat into the stillness within.

It is here, in this calm and sacred space, that you can reconnect with yourself, find clarity, and restore balance.

The journey inward is not about escaping the world, but about discovering a deep reservoir of peace that strengthens you to face it.

Children – Thank You for the Front Row Seat:

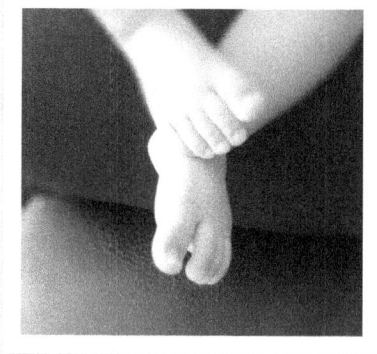

People often say that children should be grateful to their parents – for the sacrifices, the sleepless nights, the endless lessons.

But the truth is, it's we, the parents, who should be saying thank you. Not out of duty or tradition, but out of awe.

Our children didn't come into our lives just to be shaped by us – they came to reshape *us*. To open our eyes wider, stretch our hearts further, and remind us how much beauty still exists in this world.

Before they arrived, life may have felt orderly, predictable – even monochrome. But the moment they entered it, everything shifted. Someone once told me that before you have kids, the world is black and white. Afterward, it explodes into colour. And it's true. The days become fuller, the emotions deeper, the small things brighter. Their laughter becomes music, their curiosity becomes your teacher, their joy becomes your compass.

We've had the privilege – no, the miracle – of a front row seat to watch these little souls grow. To see them stumble, stand, run. To watch them fall in love with life in their own way. And in doing so, they hold a mirror up to us – showing us who we really are, who we were, and sometimes, who we forgot to be.

Yes, there are hard moments. Exhausting nights. Days where you question if you're doing anything right. But then you look back, and you realise, those little hands held yours as you became someone new. A better version. A more open-hearted, more curious, more vulnerable version of yourself.

So no, it's not our children who owe us gratitude.

It is we who owe them everything.

True Friendships:

"The reality is that many people are not deep.
They entertain connections for the sake of it, superficial reasons, practical reasons,
and, in many ways, selfish reasons.

*They don't appreciate you for **you**.*
Or maybe they do, but they don't profoundly care about you.
They might value what you can do for them or enjoy your company –
when and how it suits them and them only.

If you have depth and connect at a soul level, you may engage in these connections,
but please, be mindful not to overplay your role.
Observe who truly cares for you on a deeper level. Who cares about your happiness
and well-being?
Who makes selfless efforts for you?
Who supports you without a hidden agenda?
Who prioritises you – not just when they're bored, not just in passing, but because
they genuinely value your presence.
Because, sadly, in my experience… those people are rare."

– **Aline Frisch**, via Instagram

Friends of Convenience vs. Friends of Character:

"Most of your friends aren't really your friends.

They're just along for the ride when it's fun, convenient, or valuable.

Your real friends are the ones who are there for you when it's none of those – when you have nothing to offer in return."

Friendship reveals its truth not when life is easy, but when it's hard – when there's nothing to gain, no spotlight to share, and no comfort to offer. Friends of convenience show up for the good times, for the benefits, the laughter, the ease. They walk beside you when the road is smooth. But friends of character are different. They stay when the path gets rough, when you're no longer useful to them, when your only offering is your presence in pain.

These are the people who don't need a reason to care – they simply do. And in a world full of conditional connections, their loyalty is quiet, steady, and rare. Time may blur many bonds, but hardship always sharpens the difference between those who came for the ride and those who came for *you*.

The Enduring Power of Friendships:

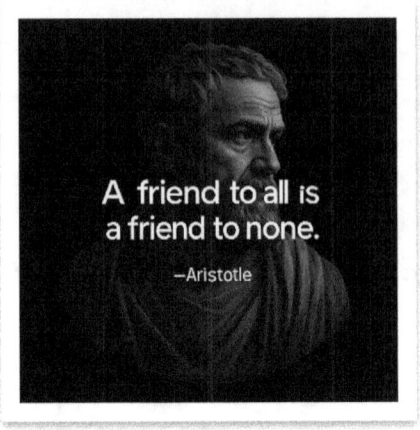

In modern times, friendships are often fluid and shallow, with people finding it far too easy to move on. The depth that once defined relationships seems to be fading, replaced by convenience and transient connections. This lack of depth in both people and relationships is something that weighs heavily on my heart because, at my core, friendships are who I am.

The friendships I treasure most are those I've nurtured for over 30 years. These relationships aren't just about shared moments or common interests – they are rooted in growth, vulnerability, and mutual respect. My closest friends have seen me at my best and my worst, and yet, we stand by each other through it all. They challenge me to be better, listen to my struggles, and offer support that goes beyond surface-level conversations.

True friendships are built on honesty and emotional investment. They offer a space for real feedback, a refuge for vulnerability, and a foundation of unwavering support, no matter the season. The essence of these friendships is not in the number of days we've spent together, but in the depth we've cultivated through years of genuine connection.

In a world where relationships are often disposable, I believe we should hold onto those rare, deep friendships that shape us, challenge us, and remind us of the richness of human connection. They are the true treasures in a world that increasingly lacks substance.

The Truth about Reciprocity and Respect:

> My personality attracts people because I'm authentic, but soon it scares them away, because I demand authenticity as well.

Relationships are based on reciprocity, we only have the ability to rely on what others provide, but be mindful of takers and energy vampires, they have no limits and get upset when you establish boundaries.

Everyone loves you when you let everything slide, but the moment you start setting boundaries and holding people accountable, you become the one that's difficult.

Everyone wants a strong network of successful friends. Until they realise that those successful friends come with standards, integrity, discipline, priorities and boundaries. People who can't deal with this then show you their narcissistic, controlling and manipulative side!

Finding Your People:

My father once told me:

"If you want to go for a run, just run.
Don't wait for company. The right people
will find you along the way."

This applies to everything in life.

Move first.
Like-minded people will follow.

Giving People Too Much Attention:

When we lavish too much attention on someone, we risk inflating their sense of self beyond reality.

Attention is a form of power. When wielded without care, it can distort identities and create illusions of greatness where none truly exist. It's a reminder that not all attention is nourishing – sometimes, it enables delusion.

True strength grows from honest reflection, humility, and grounded understanding, not from the loud echoes of excessive praise.

Friendship Groups:

"One of us will see all the funerals,
one of us will see none,
and
one will have none of us at theirs."

Friendship groups are a bond that stretches across time and life's inevitable changes.

Some of us will be there to witness every goodbye, every funeral, feeling the weight of loss deeply. Others may be spared that sorrow, while sadly, one among us might face the hardest truth – going through those moments alone, with none of us by their side.

This reality reminds us to cherish the moments we have together, to hold each other close, and to be present – not just in life's joys, but in its deepest pains.

True friendship is standing together, even when the road grows dark.

This was written for one friendship group in mind – a group that spent many Saturday nights together – you know who you are!

Your Circle of Friends:

In life, one of the most profound choices you will ever make is who you allow into your circle.

People may claim to love you, but the truth often lies in how they react to your growth. Some will judge you for changing, for outgrowing old habits or even old relationships.

Others will celebrate your ambitions, encouraging you to become the best version of yourself.

The circle you choose is a direct reflection of the future you're crafting. It's not just about who supports you when it's convenient or easy, but about who stands by you when you're pushing toward the next level. Your environment – who you associate with – shapes your mindset, your actions, and eventually, your destiny.

As Dana Peña wisely said,

> *"Show me your friends and I'll show you your future."*

The company you keep plays a significant role in determining not just where you end up, but who you become along the way.
Choose wisely, for your circle will either lift you higher or keep you tethered to where you've already been.

> The world is full of people who are grabbing and self-seeking. So the rare individual who unselfishly tries to serve others has an enormous advantage.
>
> **DALE CARNEGIE**

High Standards, Small Circles:

"Have the courage to set standards – do not accept second best, walk away from situations or relationships that are not good enough for you!"

When you set standards, you carve out a unique frequency – a vibration that resonates only with a select few. Much like a vegetarian seeking a place to eat in a town filled mostly with meat-serving restaurants, or a vegan narrowing choices even further, raising your personal standards naturally limits the circle of those who truly align with you.

This is not a limitation but a clarity. It reveals the truth that not all companionships are meant to be – nor should they be. To surround yourself with those who share your values, your integrity, and your vision requires courage. It demands patience and discernment. Because as your standards rise, the comfort of widespread approval gives way to the profound intimacy of genuine connection.

The path is narrow, but it is rich. The few who meet your frequency become your true tribe – those with whom you share not only time, but authenticity and depth. So have the courage to set your standards high. In doing so, you honour your own soul and invite others to rise to meet you – not because of expectation, but because of shared resonance.

In a world of many, be rare. Be intentional. And watch how the right connections transform your life.

Be Careful of Your Crowd:

The Unexpected Roots of True Support:

True support often arrives from unexpected places – not always from the familiar faces we've known since childhood. The friends we grew up with may not always cheer the loudest or stand the closest. Those we believed would be unwavering pillars might fade away when life demands more than surface loyalty. This truth can sting, but it is also a quiet liberation.

Sometimes, the truest allies are strangers who recognised your worth long before you believed in it yourself. They saw potential in you when others only saw the ordinary. They reached out without obligation, drawn by a connection deeper than history – a meeting of spirit and possibility.

These are the friendships forged not by time, but by understanding, respect, and shared journey. They arrive precisely because you needed them, often when you least expected it. To keep these people close is to honour the mysterious grace that brings the right souls together, reminding us that belonging is not always about roots, but about resonance.

Respect, Effort, Honesty – Non-Negotiables:

> I'm at a point in my life where I no longer have expectations, I have requirements. Respect my time. Match my effort. Keep your word. Always be honest. Stay consistent. Those are my requirements, not expectations. Requirements.

Listening – The Heartbeat of Being Human:

Listening is more than just hearing words; it is the very essence of connection and understanding that defines us as human beings.

True listening unfolds in layers – starting with the words themselves, but moving deeper into the content, the energy behind the voice, and the silent language of the body.

To listen fully, we must attune to the context – the history and emotions shaping each moment. We discern the patterns that reveal recurring truths, and we become sensitive to what remains unspoken, the gaps filled with meaning. Listening is not passive; it is an active dance of attention where even the pauses speak volumes, each silence a whispered word.

When we listen with our gut, balancing intuition with presence, we engage in a dialogue beyond words.

This depth of listening fosters empathy, strengthens relationships, and breathes life into communication. For in listening – not just speaking – we find the true heart of human engagement.

Disconnected – A Moment Outside of the Noise:

I saw a guy at a coffee shop today:

No phone

No tablet

No laptop

He just sat there drinking coffee

Like a psychopath...

Bridging the Gap – From Judgement to Understanding:

"We judge others by their actions, but ourselves by our intentions."

We live in a world where intentions and actions often stand at odds – especially in how we judge ourselves and others. We excuse our missteps with the cushion of our intentions: *I meant well, I didn't mean to hurt anyone, I was doing my best.* Yet when others falter, we rarely offer them the same softness. We hold them to the visible standard of their actions, forgetting that beneath those actions may lie struggles, fears, or quiet efforts we will never fully see.

This double standard is not a flaw in character, but a blind spot in perspective. It is easier to justify from within than to understand from without. But what if we chose to narrow that gap? What if we extended to others the same grace we so readily give ourselves? To do so is to walk the path of deeper empathy – to see not just what was done, but to wonder why. Not to excuse harm, but to hold space for complexity.

The world softens when we remember that most people, like us, are simply trying to find their way. It takes conscious effort to pause judgement and ask:

"What might I not see here?"

In that pause lies the chance to transform division into understanding, and separation into compassion.

The Persuasive Paradox – Less Is More:

As a management consultant for 30+ years, guiding global corporations through complex change journeys, I came to realise that the most persuasive leaders and influencers are often the ones who speak the least. I saw first-hand how the most effective change-makers didn't come in with grand speeches, bullet-pointed solutions, or hard-nosed directives.

Instead, they listened.

They really listened.

They wanted the people in the room to be heard.

They were experts at observing the dynamics in the room, at reading between the lines, and at understanding the emotions and fears that often drive decisions in corporate environments. More often than not, the real change wasn't achieved through presenting the perfect plan, but by creating space for others to see their own potential and work through their own answers.

The greatest persuasive force I saw was not the one who dictated what should happen, but the one who asked the right questions at the right time. It wasn't about telling others how things should change – it was about creating the environment for them to realise why change was necessary.

I learned that people don't buy into what you say – they buy into what they feel they've discovered on their own. By stepping back and not forcing an agenda, I found that my role as a consultant wasn't to be the loudest voice in the room, but to guide the conversation, to ask thoughtful questions that prompted deeper reflection, and to foster an environment where the client could come to their own conclusions.

In the world of management consulting, where agendas can be tight, expectations high, and everyone's busy, I realised that true persuasion lies in restraint. The less you say, the more others will hear – and more importantly, the more likely they are to act on it.

Flattery Is the Easy Option:

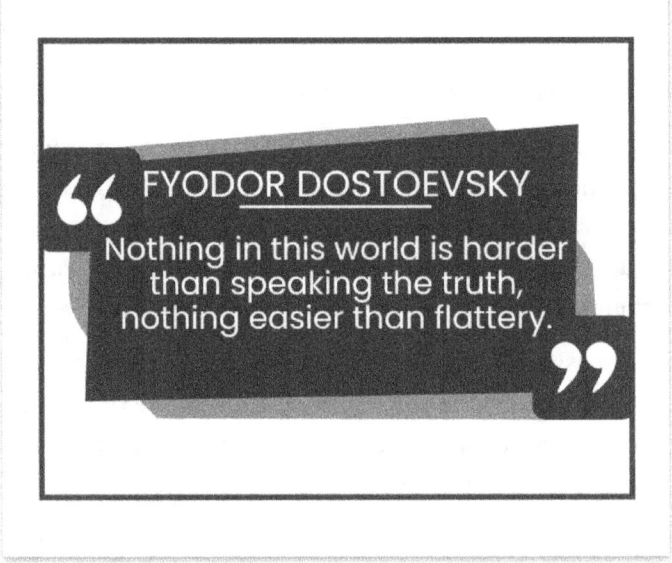

Why Do People Dislike Others?:

I have observed this all my life and have concluded that despite people holding themselves to a higher standard of integrity and friendship they may face challenges on the way.

It boils down to this:

```
         5 REASONS PEOPLE
             HATE YOU

  THEY WANT TO BE YOU, BUT CAN'T      $0.00
  MATCH YOU

  YOUR CONFIDENCE REMINDS THEM OF     $0.00
  THEIR INSECURITIES

  YOU'RE DOING WHAT THEY'RE TOO       $0.00
  AFRAID TO TRY

  YOUR SUCCESS SHINES A LIGHT ON      $0.00
  THEIR STAGNATION

  THEY CAN'T CONTROL YOU, SO THEY     $0.00
  TRY TO DISCREDIT YOU

     TOTAL                            $0.00

  *******************************
```

The Art of Not Oversharing:

Avoiding oversharing is essential for protecting your emotional well-being and fostering genuine relationships. Oversharing can leave you vulnerable, draining your energy and exposing parts of yourself that deserve care and discretion. To master the art of thoughtful communication, pause before speaking and consider whether your words serve the moment or satisfy an inner need. Set clear boundaries around what remains sacred and private, preserving both your dignity and energy.

True connection grows not from unguarded confession but from deep listening and intentional sharing. Reflect on why you might feel the urge to overshare – is it for validation, attention, or connection? – and seek those needs wisely. Use a mental filter to weigh how your words will land, favouring neutral ground over emotional excess. Prepare gentle ways to redirect conversations and tailor your openness based on the trust you hold.

By choosing what to share with intention, you maintain your dignity and build trust. Conversations become balanced exchanges – a dance, not a monologue – that protect your inner world while creating space for authentic bonds to grow. Ultimately, mastering this art helps you preserve your essence, engage meaningfully, and cultivate relationships rooted in respect and understanding.

A Key Moment in a Friendship:

"The best way to identify

a great friend is

how they react when

you win

or

you tell them

one of your successes."

A true test of friendship lies not in times of struggle, but in the quiet moments when you share your victories.

A great friend celebrates your success without envy or doubt – they rejoice genuinely, as if it were their own triumph. In that reaction, you see the depth of their heart: unshaken by jealousy, rooted in love and support.

For friendship is not competition – it is a shared journey where one's light only makes the other shine brighter.

The True Measure of Friendship?:

In the search for true friendship, we often find ourselves asking, "How many true friends do I have?"

But perhaps this is the wrong question to ask.

The measure of friendship, after all, isn't in the count of friends you have but in the quality of the friendships you've built. The true value lies not in receiving, but in giving.

Instead, ask yourself:

"How many people have you been a true friend to?"

Part III: Growth, Grit & Personal Mastery

Themes: Discipline, Resilience, Progress, Self-Belief

The Courage to Actively Live Life:

Do not stand at the edge of life, content to observe its unfolding as though it were a performance meant only for others.

There is no wisdom in passivity, no depth gained from mere observation. Life does not yield its meaning to those who sit safely on the sidelines, analysing from afar.

As the old adage reminds us:

"You can't learn to swim by reading about it."

Nor by speaking of it endlessly, nor by theorising its depths. At some point, the thinking must give way to doing – the contemplation to courage. One must step beyond the familiar shore and enter the current of lived experience.

It is only by immersion that the soul begins to understand. Risk, discomfort, vulnerability – these are the true teachers. Life invites not spectators, but participants. To delay is to deny oneself the full measure of becoming.

So leap – not recklessly, but earnestly. Let the unknown wash over you. That is how you learn to swim. That is how you begin to live.

Wanting Is Not Enough:

Manifestation and desire are not enough to bring your goals to life. While envisioning success can be powerful, many people find themselves yearning for success, recognition, or transformation, but few are willing to embrace the effort those outcomes require.

As James Clear wisely puts it:

> *"It doesn't make sense to continue wanting something if you're not willing to do what it takes to get it. If you don't want to live the lifestyle, then release yourself from the desire. To crave the result, but not the process, is to guarantee disappointment."*

This quote highlights a fundamental truth: desire alone is not enough. Without aligning our actions and habits with our ambitions, we set ourselves up for frustration and failure. True fulfilment comes when our work ethic matches our aspirations.

Dreams That Drive You:

> "DREAM IS NOT THAT WHICH YOU SEE WHILE SLEEPING; IT IS SOMETHING THAT DOES NOT LET YOU SLEEP."
> — DR. ABDUL KALAM

The Power of Action Over Words:

In a world overflowing with words and appearances, it is easy to mistake noise for meaning, or intention for progress. Yet there is a profound and enduring truth: **only action carries weight**.

We often busy ourselves with the illusion of momentum, engaging in activities that mimic purpose without ever confronting the discipline of execution.

Consider:

- Preparing to do the work is not doing the work.
- Scheduling time is not the same as showing up.
- Telling others what you plan to do is not taking a single step.
- Messaging peers – regardless of their own efforts – does not move you forward.
- Criticising those who have achieved what you desire will never bring you closer to it.
- Dreaming of success is not success.
- Fantasising about the applause that may follow action is still not action.

Only doing the thing is doing the thing.

To possess knowledge and never apply it is like owning a seed you never plant, or guarding a flame you never ignite. Action is the bridge between potential and reality – between who we are and who we might become.

Be Mindful of Your Frequency:

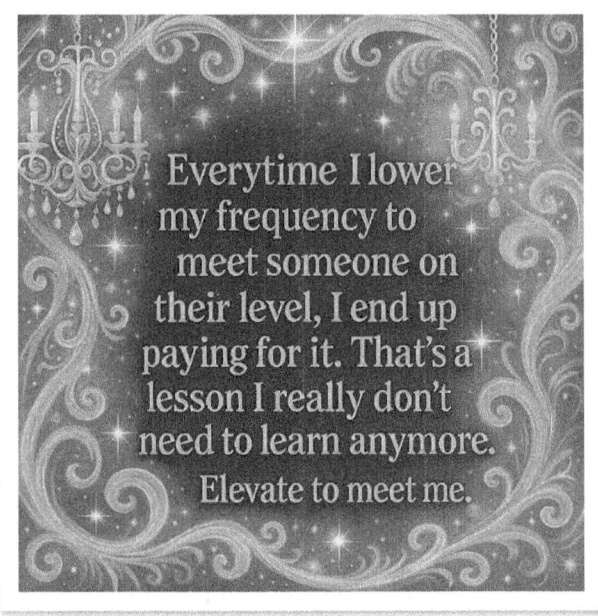

You Set Your Own Limits:

You are the one who sets your own limits – no one else can define what you're truly capable of. So aim high, dream boldly, and believe in your potential.

Surround yourself with people who uplift you, challenge you, and believe in your vision.

With the right support and a fearless mindset, you won't just reach new heights – you'll soar far beyond them.

Embracing Growth – Navigating Unintended Challenges:

When you start living and acting differently from the masses, it makes everyone uncomfortable.

The fact that you no longer play the same game of showing off, massaging egos, fear and drama like you were conditioned to, makes everyone aware of their own limitations and insecurities.

When you operate on an authentic frequency underpinned with humility, people don't know how to approach you because you outgrow their energy and their level of capabilities (i.e., their level of consciousness).

When you are different, people don't know where to fit you anymore; your existence transcends their preconceived ideas.

You won't be able to meet people's expectations anymore because you're not the same person anymore and you no longer operate on the same frequencies.

They will judge you for being different and for what they believe is playing out.

You will not judge them as you understand them at a deeper level and the context and parameters in which they are operating.

"Embrace your growth, maintain your humility, your authenticity

And the right people will be attracted and embrace the new you!"

Not Fulfilling Your Potential Is Terrifying:

Read the title again and let it sink in for a moment.

Your potential should terrify you. Not fulfilling your potential should terrify you.

Not because your potential is out of reach.

But because it's there for the taking.

You've seen glimpses of it yourself. In the rare moments you actually believe in yourself, you actually let loose and you go all in.

Deep down, you know what would happen if you stopped playing small, gave it everything and played to win!

That thought is what scares you – not failure.

But the fact that you're capable of so much more – it's like owning a Ferrari and refusing to shift out of first gear.

And every day you don't act on it, you feel it. It may be quiet but it weighs on you every moment of every day.

It's like a life you were supposed to live is waiting for you to show up.

"Wake up, smell the coffee and show up. It's that simple."

Taking Accountability for Your Life:

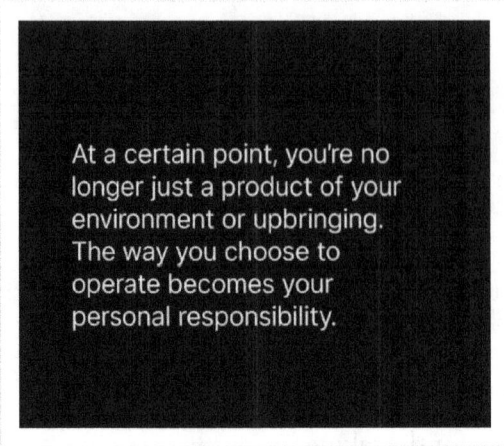

You are the author of your own story. No one can live your life for you – only you can shape it.

- Doctors can guide you to health, but the choices you make about your body are yours.
- Teachers can offer knowledge, but the effort to learn is up to you.
- Trainers can provide a workout plan, but the sweat and effort needed to get fit come from you.
- Coaches can share strategies, but the drive to succeed lies within you.

Life doesn't just happen to you – it's your responsibility. Stop waiting for someone else to change your circumstances.

Your success, your health, your happiness – they are your personal responsibility.

Own it.

Attributes of Great Leaders:

Over the past 30 years advising the Boards of multinational corporations, I have had the privilege of working closely with some truly exceptional leaders. While each brings their own unique approach and personality, certain core traits consistently distinguish those who lead at the highest level. These qualities are rarely innate – they are cultivated through experience, self-awareness, and a relentless drive for growth.

The most outstanding leaders I've encountered tend to share the following attributes:

- **Gravitas** – a natural presence and ability to command the room
- **Inspirational leadership** – they earn deep loyalty; their teams would "walk through walls" for them
- **Strategic influence** – they know how to frame and sell ideas effectively at board level
- **Clarity of thought** – they distil complex, nuanced issues into clear, actionable insights
- **Competitive drive** – an insatiable hunger to succeed and deliver results
- **Political acumen** – an instinctive ability to read people and navigate organisational dynamics
- **Risk intelligence** – a clear understanding of calculated risk and its role in driving growth
- **Cultural embodiment** – they don't just represent the organisation's values – they live them.

People Who Don't Follow the Crowd:

"What the herd hates most is the one who thinks and acts differently; it is not so much the opinion or act itself, but the audacity of wanting to think or act for themselves, something that they do not know how to do."

— Arthur Schopenhauer

This quote has had a significant impact on me. People often don't get upset because someone has a different opinion or takes a different path – they get upset because that person had the courage to think and act for themselves.

Independent thinking can feel threatening to those who are used to following the crowd. It's not the idea that bothers them, but the reminder that they're not choosing for themselves.

This quote is a reminder that being true to yourself takes courage, especially when others fear that kind of freedom.

Another famous quote on herd mentality is from Nietzsche.

"The Rise of the Herd."

– Friedrich Nietzsche

In Nietzsche's view, modern society had become a herd – not a community of strong individuals, but a mass of people trained to move together, think alike, and avoid standing out.

Nietzsche had a name for this: slave morality. And what does the herd praise most?

- Niceness over honesty
- Safety over growth
- Agreement over truth
- Obedience over courage

Both Nietzsche and Schopenhauer capture the drivers of human psychology so well and articulate it in a way that should give us the strength to be true to ourselves in both our personal and professional lives. There is no other way to live your life!

Don't Be an Ironing Board:

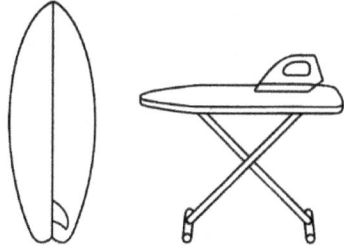

Trapped in the Eyes of Others:

At its core, the quote suggests that **we often surrender our own views to meet the standards set by others**, not because we are forced, but because we internalise those expectations.

This quote challenges us to examine which expectations truly serve us, and which ones we're clinging to out of fear.

To reflect more personally, ask:

- Whose approval am I still chasing?
- What parts of myself have I hidden to "fit in"?
- If I dropped others' expectations, what might I finally do, or become?

Freedom begins when we see the bars – and realise we hold the key.

The Power of Repetition:

> Your subconscious mind learns through repetition, not logic. Tell it who you are until it has no choice but to believe.

This is why you must be careful – where you spend your time, how you constantly speak to yourself, and where you place your energy.

What you repeat becomes who you are.

The Philosophy of Becoming Exceptional:

This paradox reveals a deep tension within the human spirit: the desire for greatness coupled with the reluctance to stand apart.

To truly grow, one must embrace the courage to be an exception – to resist the currents of conformity and instead chart a course defined by deliberate choice and unwavering self-belief. The future self is not a mere destination to be discovered; it is a creation, forged by the intentional acts of today.

Who you become in ten years is shaped not by chance, but by the food you consume, the company you keep, the habits you nurture, the knowledge you pursue, the risks you dare to take, and the standards you steadfastly uphold.

Work-life balance does not cross the minds of those striving to excel. They understand the level of effort that must be sustained, and they have consciously prioritised the journey over comfort or convention. This is not a rejection of balance, but a redefinition of it – where the scales are tipped, for a season or a lifetime, in favour of purpose, discipline, and personal evolution.

This journey also demands high agency – the recognition that your destiny is in your hands, moulded choice by choice. To follow the crowd while yearning for different outcomes is folly; true transformation requires stepping beyond the familiar, becoming the exception you aspire to be.

The future is not a gift to be found, but something to be built – moment by moment – through a huge amount of effort, conscious growth and courageous individuality.

Success Is a Game – Learn How to Play:

Success isn't just about hard work, treat work like a game. The game takes years to master and will have ups and downs. Key attributes to develop:

- **Leaning in**: Hard work opens doors and creates luck.
- **Find great leaders**: Work under leaders who inspire you; great leaders seek great team players.
- **Be agile**: Work with different teams, understand them, and build bridges. Cross-functional expertise is invaluable.
- **Positive attitude**: No one wants to work with complainers.
- **Keep personal matters private**: Colleagues are not your friends; maintain professionalism.
- **Own clients**: Be client-facing so they follow you if you leave. Your value comes from relationships, not back-office roles.
- **Make decisions for the company and clients**: Prioritize what's best for them over personal interests.
- **Visibility**: Great employees position themselves to be seen, heard, and valued.
- **Develop commercial skills**: Be pragmatic and make things happen. Don't wait for direction.
- **Balance work**: Enjoy the game, but remember, work isn't life.
- **Build a thick skin:** It's rarely personal at work. How you handle setbacks determines your success.
- **Seek progress:** When leaders recognise your value, ask for a promotion. If you don't ask, you won't get.
- **You set your limits**: No one else does.

Self-Belief – The Great Divider:

There is a silent tyranny that governs many lives – not the tyranny of others, but of self-doubt. It is the internal whisper that says, "Not yet," or worse, "Not you." And yet, as George Mack reminds us: *"There is someone who has half your talent, with five times your self-belief and ten times your earnings."* This is not just a commentary on wealth. It's an indictment of potential left unrealised, and of brilliance waiting for permission.

Self-belief is not arrogance. It is not a delusion of grandeur or a denial of flaws. It is the quiet conviction that you are allowed to try, to fail, to rise, and to try again. It is the engine behind courage, the currency of creation, the spark behind all meaningful risk.

The difference between belief and doubt is not always in ability, but in posture – how we stand in the face of the unknown. Nowhere is this more visible than in the cultural psychology of ambition. In the UK, there is often an invisible ceiling built from fear of embarrassment, from the ingrained tendency to *play not to lose*. Across the Atlantic, in the American mindset, there is a different rhythm: a boldness that *plays to win*, sometimes brashly, but often effectively.

This is not to say one is right and the other wrong. But the lesson is there, stark as day. A lesser mind with greater belief will often go further than the gifted one who hesitates.

So the challenge is simple and immense: Believe first. Do second. And let the world catch up to your conviction. Because if someone with half your talent can achieve more, the issue was never talent – it was trust in yourself.

Being Flexible to Life's External Factors:

"When the music changes, so does the dance."

– African Proverb

Life is full of twists and turns.

Just like a dancer adjusts to a new beat, we have to adapt when circumstances change. Holding on to the past or resisting change only makes things harder.

Whether it's in business, relationships, or personal growth, those who stay flexible and open-minded are the ones who thrive. Change isn't something to fear, it's an invitation to move forward.

This mindset is at the heart of *Who Moved My Cheese?*, one of the most successful business books of all time, which illustrates through a simple yet profound story that agility is not just beneficial – it's vital.

The characters who thrive are the ones willing to let go of old expectations, stay alert to their environment, and adapt quickly when the "cheese" – their source of comfort or success – moves.

The book reinforces the idea that change is inevitable, and resisting it only leads to frustration and stagnation. Just like the dancer who must stay in rhythm with the music, we must stay in rhythm with life. Agility, awareness, and a willingness to act are the keys to not just surviving change, but embracing it as the path to new opportunities.

Mastering a Craft – Finding Your Space in the World:

<u>*Tesla:*</u>

Nikola Tesla often worked from 3 am to 11 pm and claimed he only needed two hours of sleep. He frequently forgot to eat – too consumed by his inventions to care.

<u>*Beethoven:*</u>

Beethoven was known to go days without eating or changing clothes while composing. He went completely deaf and still kept creating masterpieces.

<u>*Da Vinci:*</u>

Da Vinci filled over 7,000 pages with sketches, ideas, and inventions – most of which no one ever saw. He wasn't chasing recognition. He was chasing mastery.

<u>*Michelangelo:*</u>

Michelangelo slept in his clothes and rarely bathed while painting the Sistine Chapel. He spent four years with his neck craned toward the ceiling – lost in the work.

<u>*Stanley Kubrick:*</u>

Stanley Kubrick often demanded over 100 takes for a single scene. He once made actors redo a shot for four straight days – just to get the *right feel*.

These weren't just acts of discipline. They were acts of devotion.

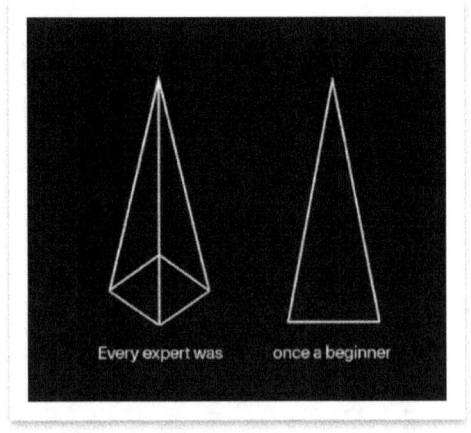

Create First, Perfect Later:

The Price of Greatness:

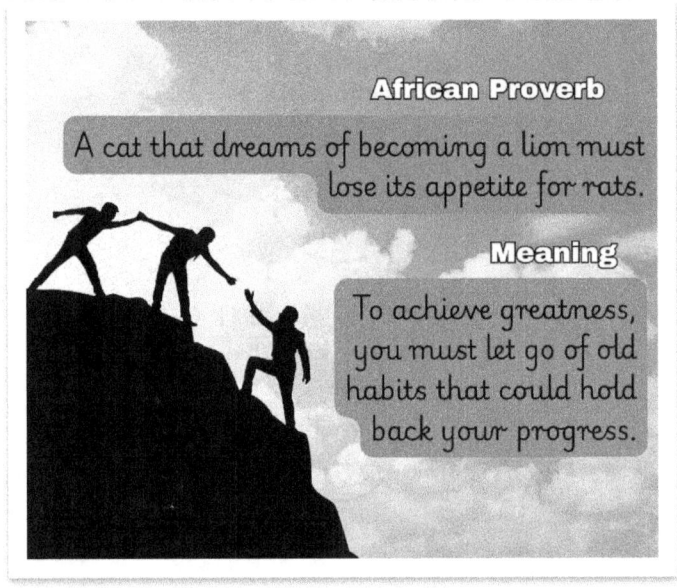

Growth – From Ego to Evolution:

"If you cannot be corrected without taking offence, you are not ready to grow."

Growth isn't easy. It's raw, disruptive, and uncomfortable. But if you're holding this book, you're drawn to it – you want more for yourself. For the past 17 years, I've been mentored by John Mullins, former COO of Herbert Smith Freehills. He never sugarcoated the truth. He didn't coddle me, and I'm stronger for it. That's what growth looks like: **not self-improvement, but self-confrontation.**

It's the breaking down of ego to make room for evolution. Correction, when given with truth and care, isn't criticism – it's clarity. But to accept it, you have to choose truth over comfort.

"If someone can prove me wrong, I shall gladly change. I seek the truth, which never harmed anyone."

– Marcus Aurelius

I've worked with many who say they want to grow but resist the things that make it possible: feedback, challenge, accountability. You cannot evolve while protecting a self-image built on comfort and denial. Correction is a compass that redirects you. Those who offer it honestly and kindly are not threats to your peace. They're defenders of your potential, loving you enough to risk your approval.

Ego hides behind the mask of confidence, afraid of being wrong. True strength is found in humility – the quiet power to admit, "I was wrong," and ask, "How can I grow?"

A Poem – The Curse of Competence:

"If you are good at things, and have high standards,
you assume that you should always do well.

Which means that success isn't a form of celebration,
but it's the minimum level of reasonable performance.

Anything less than victory would be a failure, and
victory itself becomes nothing more than acceptable.

Congratulations.

You might be very successful,
you also might be miserable."

– Chris Williamson

Weathering the Storm – Roger Federer, and the Art of the Moment:

Roger Federer, a Swiss tennis player often regarded as one of the greatest athletes in the history of sport, was more than a champion – he was a philosophy in motion.

With 20 Grand Slam titles, 310 weeks as the world No. 1, and a style defined by elegance, Federer redefined excellence. Yet for all his glory, the numbers tell a humbling story: over the course of his luminous career, he won only 54% of the points he played. Just slightly more than half.

By the calculus of success, the margins appear unremarkable. But Federer's greatness was never about domination – it was about discernment. He knew that mastery isn't the elimination of error, but the refinement of response. A lost point was not a crisis – it was to be weathered. He did not resist it; he let it pass.

His gift was presence, a kind of temporal grace. He played the moment, not the memory. There's a lesson here beyond tennis. Life, like Federer's game, unfolds in fragments – half chances, near misses, points barely won. We stumble through heartbreak, rejection, uncertainty.

To live well is not to win everything. It is to know which moments to meet with everything we have.

– Inspired by Roger Federer's 2024 commencement speech at Dartmouth College

Beyond the Hammer – A Philosophy of Perception and Value:

Abraham Maslow once observed:

"If the only tool you have is a hammer, it is tempting to treat everything as if it were a nail."

In the world of modern management and consulting, this metaphor rings louder than ever.

For over three decades, I have watched organisations, leaders, and industries approach every challenge with the same predictable arsenal: increase efficiency, reduce costs, optimise performance. These tools are sharpened and effective – but they are not universal keys. They solve only the problems that fit within their narrow frame. Worse still, they risk flattening what is rich, human, and intangible into something measurable, transactional, and ultimately, diminished.

The tragedy is not that efficiency is valued, but that it is often **overvalued** – elevated as the only lens through which decisions are made. In doing so, we overlook the silent pillars that hold deeper meaning: the heritage of a company, the spirit of its people, the story embedded in its culture, and the non-linear, immeasurable value of trust, creativity, and identity.

When we treat every problem like a nail, we not only misapply force – we miss the nuance. We forget that some things are not meant to be streamlined, but stewarded. Some systems thrive not through reduction, but through preservation. Some values, though unquantifiable, are what give a business – or a life – its soul.

To truly lead, we must widen our conceptual toolkit.

Your Future Self:

> **BREATHE. YOU HAVEN'T MET ALL OF YOU YET. THERE IS SO MUCH MORE LIFE TO LIVE.**

There is a quiet mercy in not knowing everything you are becoming. Like the ocean tide that reshapes the shore grain by grain, your future self is still forming – sometimes beneath the surface, where your eyes cannot follow. The struggles you carry today, the questions that press against your chest like heavy stone, are not endpoints. They are chisels in the sculptor's hands.

Every breath you take is a vote for continuation, for possibility. You are not a fixed point in time but a passage, a becoming. There are strengths in you still sleeping, loves not yet kindled, wisdom that will only arise when time and experience stretch far enough to call them forth.

Do not be so quick to define yourself by your current state.

You are not finished. You are not final.

So, breathe.

Give yourself permission to evolve, to surprise yourself.

The Price of Authentic Maturity:

One of the hardest parts of maturing is realising you won't vibe with most people. You won't be part of the hive mentality.

You're more loyal to your soul instead of society. Too real to fake fitting in. You don't feel the need to explain yourself.

Don't be discouraged. It's better to wait for those who resonate with you at a soul level than to force connections that dim your light.

Don't trade in your truth for a little validation or attention. Enjoy your sacred solitude and remain authentic. And you'll become more **magnetic** to the ones who are genuinely in tune with your unique vibrational frequency.

Embody who you are – fully. As a result, you will attract those meant to walk beside you.

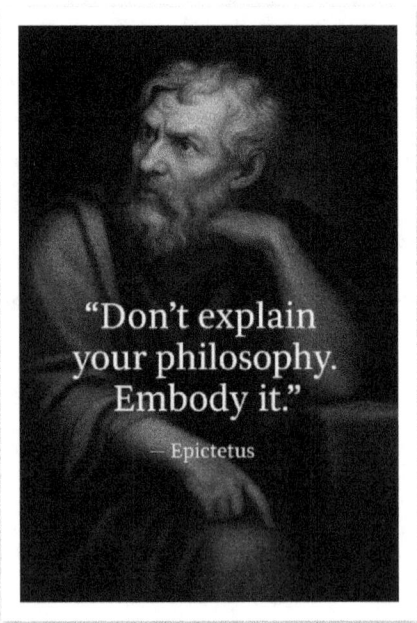

The Inner Hell of the Unrealised Self:

"The definition of hell – when the person you are meets the person you could have been."

Hell is not a fiery pit or a place of torment beyond the grave. It is a far more intimate and profound suffering – the quiet, relentless meeting of two versions of yourself: the man you are, standing face-to-face with the person you could have been.

This encounter is a mirror held up not by others, but by your own conscience. It reveals the vast terrain of potential left unexplored, the dreams abandoned, the courage unclaimed. It is a place where regret festers, not because of failure alone, but because of the choices left unmade, the risks not taken, the life unlived.

To face this hell is to confront the gap between action and intention, between who you allowed yourself to become and who you might have been in another life, another moment. Yet within this painful meeting lies a call – a call to awaken, to act, and to bridge that divide before time erodes all possibility.

Hell is not final; it is a warning. It urges us to close the distance between the man we are and the person we long to become, so that when they meet, it is not in despair, but in quiet fulfilment.

O Captain, My Captain:

"Education is bitter, but its fruit is sweet."
– Aristotle

It's a truth that arrives late in life – often too late for the young to grasp: the lessons that shape us most deeply come cloaked in boredom, resistance, or irrelevance. As children, school feels like a task to be endured rather than a gift to be embraced. For many of us, education was simply a stepping stone – a hoop to jump through on the way to somewhere else.

Only years later, far from the classroom and beyond the tests, do we see the true yield of what was planted. By the time we taste the fruit, we've already outgrown the tree we once resented. And yet – **we plant it anyway**.

Because education isn't just the transmission of facts but a slow awakening of the self. In *Dead Poets Society*, the words "**O Captain! My Captain!**" echo as a rebellion of reverence – a soul stirred from slumber. These students were learning how to live. To feel. To choose. To become.

The truly great teacher does not simply instruct – they *ignite*. They look beyond the present version of a student and speak directly to the person they could one day be. In a world obsessed with outcomes, metrics, and efficiency, the exceptional educator dares to ask the challenging questions.

This is the sacred paradox of education, its value is often invisible in the moment, misunderstood or dismissed by those it seeks to serve. But its echo resounds across a lifetime.

So we educate our children. We plant. We inspire. Not for applause, nor for instant recognition, but because we believe in the unseen harvest. One day, long after the classroom walls have faded from memory, a former student will pause – not to recall the facts they memorised, but the way they were challenged, encouraged, and awakened. And they will understand.

Maybe one day, they may even get their own book published!

Ideas in Motion:

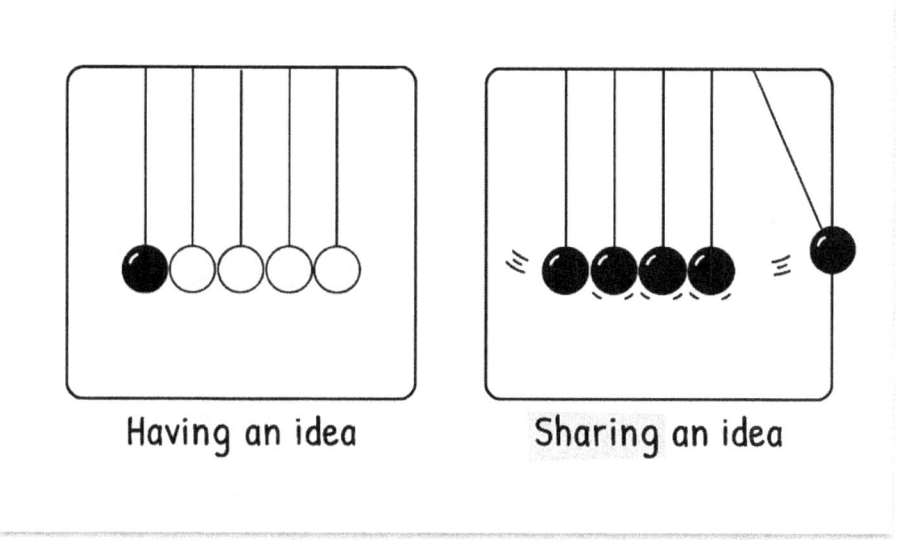

Stay Fluid, Stay Free:

Beware the moment you allow the older version of yourself to settle too deeply within. For once that weight anchors your spirit, it becomes a prison from which liberation is difficult.

To carry the past too heavily is to bind the soul, closing off the possibility of growth, renewal, and freedom. The self must remain fluid – always open to change, willing to shed old skins and embrace new horizons.

Do not let the "older you" confine the "you" that still yearns to become.

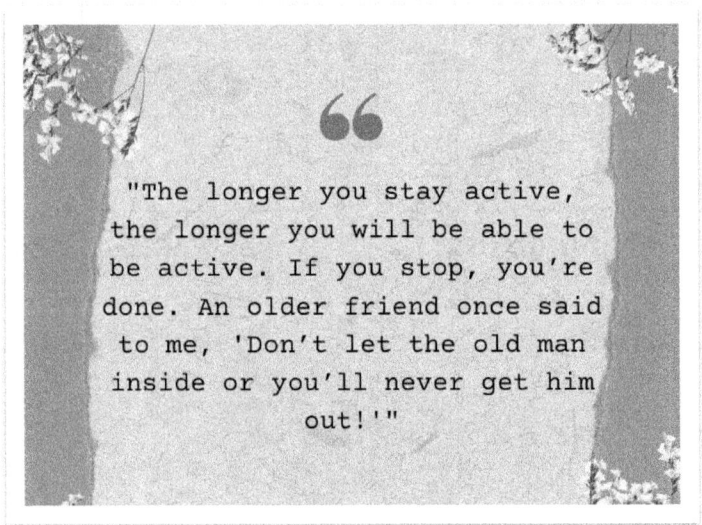

"The longer you stay active, the longer you will be able to be active. If you stop, you're done. An older friend once said to me, 'Don't let the old man inside or you'll never get him out!'"

The Trap of Mental Masturbation:

There is a subtle danger in getting lost within the mind's endless chatter – what some call mental masturbation – a seductive cycle of planning without doing. It feels productive, this constant weaving of dreams and strategies, a high on the idea of success without ever stepping into the messy, uncertain reality that leads there. Yet, this is a trap: a paralysis disguised as progress, where thought replaces action and vision overshadows movement.

Manifesting the end goal is vital, but equally vital is manifesting the steps that bring that goal to life. Real growth does not unfold in the quiet corridors of your mind – it bursts forth in the imperfect, sometimes awkward, first step taken. The mind is a powerful architect, but without execution, it builds castles in the air.

To move forward, you must shift from endless imagining to intentional doing. Stop rehearsing how your future might unfold and start building it, brick by brick. The grind – the hard, relentless, often unglamorous work – will always surpass the daydream. True progress is not a product of thought alone but of courage in action.

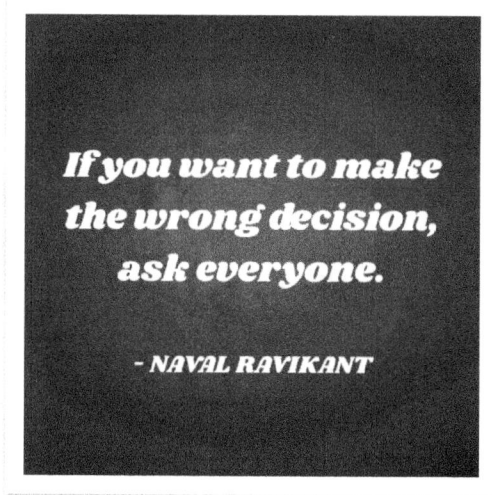

The Highest Form of Learning:

"Recognise that unlearning is the highest form of learning."

– Rumi

True growth begins not by adding more to what we know, but by bravely letting go of what we thought was certain.

Unlearning strips away the armour of old beliefs, prejudices, and fears, creating space for deeper understanding and transformation. It is the quiet courage to admit that what once served us may now limit us – and to choose freedom over comfort.

In this surrender, we discover that wisdom is not a destination but a continuous unfolding, where shedding what no longer fits is the truest path to becoming.

To unlearn is to make room for the new self, waiting patiently to emerge.

The Paradox of Effort and Recognition:

"Before you win, everyone asks you why you're working so hard and after you've won everyone asks how you got so lucky?"

– Mark Manson

Before achieving visible success, your hard work might seem excessive or even unnecessary to others. People might question your dedication, sacrifice, or ambition because they don't yet see the results. They might think you're overdoing it or chasing something unrealistic.

Once you finally succeed, those same people often dismiss your effort by attributing your success to **luck** rather than the years of hard work, sacrifice, and persistence you put in. Instead of acknowledging your discipline or commitment, they may reduce your achievement to a matter of chance or good timing.

The quote is so powerful as it is pointing out the **disconnect** between how hard work is perceived **before** results show and how success is often viewed **after** it arrives.

It's a commentary on how:

- People often fail to recognise the **grind** behind success.

- Society tends to celebrate outcomes while ignoring the process.

- Success can lead to **misinterpretation or jealousy**, where others comfort themselves by saying, *"You just got lucky,"* rather than admitting your discipline played a big role.

Stay focused and trust your process, even when others don't understand or appreciate your efforts – because people often only value results, not the journey.

The Unintended Teachers:

> I just heard someone say,
>
> "Unfortunately some people were not put here to evolve. They are here to remind you what it looks like if you don't."
>
> And it makes so much sense.

Isn't it ironic? Like living statues frozen in time, these people stand as cautionary tales at the crossroads of growth.

They show us what happens when comfort zones become tombs and stubbornness wins over curiosity. But instead of frustration, maybe we should thank them – because without their example, how else would we know what to avoid?

So here's to them – the unintentional heroes of our personal evolution, the mirrors reflecting what happens when we forget that change is the only way forward...

The Quiet Power of Compounding:

All meaningful benefits in life arise from one enduring principle: compounding.

It's the secret to lasting success in life. Just like interest grows wealth over time, small, consistent actions gradually shape every part of our lives.

- **Compounding interest** grows wealth.
- **Compounding habits** build trust in relationships.
- **Compounding effort** transforms your body.
- **Compounding care** ensures long-term health.
- **Compounding choices** shape your energy, diet, and resilience.

Nothing truly valuable happens overnight. It's built day by day, action by action.

As the philosopher Seneca said:

> *"It is not that we have a short time to live, but that we waste a lot of it."*

Compounding teaches us that growth comes from small, steady steps. By focusing on what we can improve bit by bit, over time, the results can be extraordinary.
Even a small daily improvement – like 1% – can have a huge impact. In just 100 days, you'll more than double your starting point. From 1 to 2.77.

But, **if you don't change** – if you don't grow – then nothing changes. In fact, **1 (no change)** to the power of 100 still equals **1**.

In the end, it's not about rushing but investing time wisely, one small step at a time. This is the path to lasting fulfilment.

The Long Game – In Praise of the Patient Few:

These are the rare, radiant souls who live for the long game – who pour themselves, day by day, into building lasting wisdom, enduring health, true wealth, and relationships that run soul-deep.

They're not easy to find. But when you do, don't let go. Because these people don't just touch your life – they transform it.

Their presence stretches you.

Their words light sparks in your mind.

Their quiet drive lifts your sights to places you never imagined reaching.

Being around them feels different. More intentional. More awake. Like you're finally in the presence of what really matters.

You'll learn from their triumphs, yes – but even more from their scars. From the way they carry themselves through storms. From the silent rituals of discipline they keep when no one is watching.

In a world addicted to shortcuts, compounders are a living reminder: that patience is powerful, and time – time is sacred.

– Inspired by *How to Live an Extraordinary Life* by Anthony Pompliano

The Power of Focus:

> **NOT EVERYTHING THAT DEMANDS YOUR ATTENTION DESERVES IT.**

Growth Mindset Is Everything:

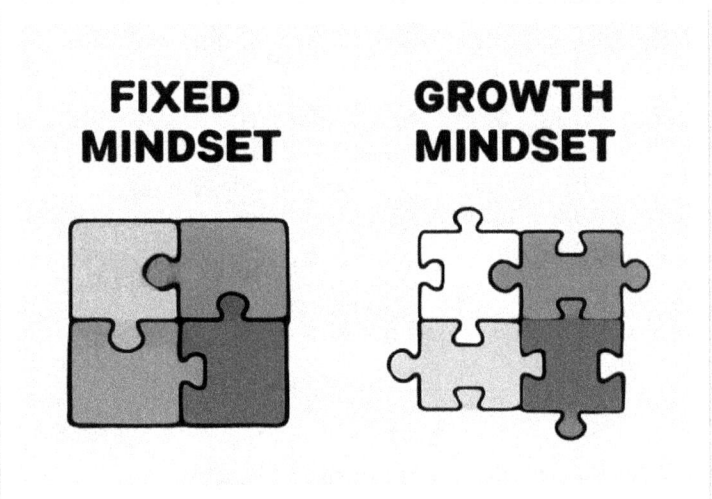

Atomic Habits and the Architecture of Change:

James Clear (author of Atomic Habits) reminds us that:

> *"You do not rise to the level of your goals. You fall to the level of your systems."*

This simple truth carries profound weight. Goals, often lofty and inspiring, are like distant stars – guiding lights that draw us forward. Yet it is the daily systems, the small repeated actions, that build the path beneath our feet.

Habits are the compound interest of personal growth. Just as a river carves a canyon drop by drop, tiny, consistent behaviours shape the contours of our character and destiny. They may seem insignificant in the moment, but over time, they accumulate powerfully, for better or worse.

In embracing the power of "atomic habits," we recognise that transformation is rarely sudden or dramatic. Instead, it unfolds quietly, patiently, through the accumulation of small choices made with intention.

The Stoics teach us a parallel truth: Marcus Aurelius urged,

> *"Waste no more time arguing what a good man should be. Be one."*

It is in the everyday, in the repeated acts of discipline and virtue, that we become who we truly aspire to be. Our systems – the rituals, the habits – are the true architects of our lives.

Embracing Your Natural Strengths:

In my executive career, leading multiple teams, strength-based development has been the core philosophy. I even used to teach a programme called *Genius, Power, and Dreams*. This has been the basis of where I stand:

What is your natural strength? What is your natural genius – what do you find easy that others struggle with? These are the key questions that unlock the path to true growth.

In a world that often promotes the idea of being well-rounded – of balancing strengths and weaknesses – the truth is that true mastery comes from doubling down on what you're naturally great at.

I ask these questions again so you think about them more deeply: what is your natural strength? What is your natural genius – what do you find easy that others struggle with?" This is your genius. It's the place where your potential is most powerful, and it's where you can make the most profound impact.

When we spend too much energy trying to "fix" our weaknesses, we risk diluting our strengths. Strengthening a weakness too much can often result in weakening what we're truly gifted at – like a professional athlete trying to become average in all areas rather than a master in one. In sports, we don't see the best basketball player trying to be equally skilled in football or tennis. They focus solely on their game, honing their craft, pushing their limits, and fine-tuning their abilities.

Similarly, in life, it's not about being good at everything, but about being exceptional at one thing that sets you apart and adds unique value to the world.

"The world does not need more well-rounded people; they need people who are great at that one thing that can make an impact."

The Power of Never Giving Up:

Your second try takes twice the emotional effort and half the actual effort

Leaning In – The Permission Illusion:

Don't wait for permission – lean fully into the moment and commit yourself without hesitation. The world does not owe you validation; it is not a gatekeeper of your becoming.

Those who shape reality do not linger in the shadows of readiness or approval. They step forward, unarmed by certainty, propelled by an inner necessity to move. To desire is to become; to hesitate is to wither. If your heart calls you to a task, answer without asking permission.

Learn through movement. Try, fail, adapt, and persist. This cycle is not merely a method – it is the essence of transformation.

The true barrier between you and what you seek is the illusion that you must be granted permission to claim it.

Consider this: when you give 80%, you receive 80%. But when you surrender yourself fully – 100% – you enter a realm where returns multiply beyond reason. That final 20% is the crucible where the ordinary fractures and the extraordinary is forged. Few possess the fierce blend of delusion, obsession, and raw vulnerability – perhaps birthed in childhood pain – that drives them beyond logic's retreat.

Here, your greatest weakness becomes your greatest strength: the refusal to stop. Success, at this juncture, ceases to be a matter of talent or fortune. It is a test of endurance – a measure of who is willing to endure the longest, to endure the pain that refines and reveals.

Pain is the filter through which only the truly committed pass.

It's Never Too Late to Begin:

We live in a world that celebrates early success, where genius is expected to shine young, and greatness is measured by how quickly someone rises. This pressure is even stronger for kids born into successful families.

But these expectations can stop the next generation from finding their own path, learning, and growing in their own time.

The truth is, the most powerful stories don't always start at the top. They often begin after years of struggle, mistakes, and growth.

Take Colonel Harland Sanders. He was 65 when he started Kentucky Fried Chicken. Before that, he'd been a farmhand, a steamboat pilot, a failed restaurateur. Yet, while others slowed down, he pushed forward and built a global brand despite having heard countless *no's*.

Vera Wang didn't design her first wedding dress until she was 40. She had tried figure skating, journalism, and fashion, but only in midlife did she find her true passion. Today, she's a symbol of elegance and proof that it's never too late to create something beautiful.

These stories aren't rare. They're reminders.

That starting late isn't failure. If you're not where you thought you'd be yet, that's okay. It means your moment is still coming.

The world may cheer the fast starters, but history remembers those who kept going – and began when they were truly ready.

Part IV: Society, Illusions & Broader Truths

Themes: Social Commentary, Wisdom, Cultural Insight

What You Inspire, They Fear:

"Remember most people don't dislike you – they dislike what you remind them they're not doing."

Sometimes the resistance you feel from others isn't about you at all. It's about the mirror you unknowingly hold up. Your courage exposes their hesitation. Your growth unsettles their comfort. Your light may illuminate the shadow they've tried to avoid.

You begin to rise – not to compete, but to become more of who you are – and suddenly, you are met with discomfort, silence, even rejection. But this is not always malice. It is fear. A quiet fear that your authenticity reminds them of the dreams they postponed, the truth they silenced, the life they haven't yet dared to live.

It is easier to criticise than to change. Easier to project than to reflect.

In a world that teaches conformity, living truthfully is revolutionary. And revolutions often make people uneasy.

But don't dim yourself to make others comfortable. Don't shrink your spirit to fit inside someone else's story. The discomfort you stir may be the very seed of someone else's awakening – even if they don't yet see it.

Stay kind. Stay steady. Stay true.

Normalise investing in your character and see how far you will go.

The Comfort Zone of Being Wrong:

In today's world of information overload, social media, and echo chambers, this quote rings truer than ever. People often hold onto their beliefs tightly, even when faced with clear evidence to the contrary.

Cognitive biases like confirmation bias make us seek information that supports what we already think, and reject anything that challenges us.

Admitting we were wrong means confronting uncomfortable truths, vulnerability, and sometimes, loss of identity or social standing. So, it's easier for someone to be misled or deceived than to accept the painful reality that they've been misled – and change their mind.

This dynamic fuels misinformation, fake news, and polarised debates, showing how deep our resistance to admitting error really is.

Your Multiplicity of Truth:

Each of us inhabits a unique world – a world shaped not by objective facts alone, but by the intricate web of our experiences, beliefs, and emotions. Our perception is a lens coloured by the joys and wounds we carry, the stories we tell ourselves, and the values we hold dear.

What resonates as truth in one heart may seem foreign or even false in another. This divergence is not a failure of understanding, but a testament to the profound complexity of human existence.

In this light, judgement becomes a fragile act. To rush to condemnation is to overlook the vastness of perspective that surrounds us. Wisdom dwells in the pause – the moment where we resist reaction and open ourselves to the possibility of other truths.

To hold firmly to one's own truth is natural; to recognise it is not the only truth is an act of humility and grace. It invites dialogue, compassion, and the expansion of the self beyond its solitary horizon.

Thus, we learn that truth is not a singular monument to be conquered, but a constellation of voices to be heard – each reflecting a facet of the human condition.

The Truth About Being Special:

One of the most honest and grounded messages ever delivered by a professional sports manager came from Luis Enrique, Head Coach of Paris Saint-Germain:

"One of the messages we've been trying to instil is: none of you are special. And if someone has made you believe you are, they are misleading you. They are fooling you. Because the moment you retire, you'll stop being 'special.' Truly special people are those who save lives, those who dedicate their entire lives to helping others. That's not us. We're just very fortunate people with a skill set that happens to be paid well."

This sentiment recently came to life for me in a deeply personal way.

At my son's school, I got to know a fellow parent – quiet, humble, and not one to talk about himself. After months of casual conversation, he eventually shared what he does: he's a surgeon who specialises in retrieving organs from deceased donors (a Transplant Physician), ensuring they can be transplanted to save the lives of those in critical need.

In a school where many parents are successful professionals: consultants, bankers, lawyers, etc., he quietly stands apart not because of status or wealth, but because of the profound impact his work has on real people every single day.

He is the kind of person that deserves to be celebrated and the one we should hold up as an example to our children.

Life Beyond the Illusion:

True success lies in knowing your worth while wearing humility as a quiet cloak. This balance is a compass guiding us beyond fears and limiting stories.

I hope you allow your life to be bigger than you ever imagined – more beautiful than you thought possible.

I hope you don't define yourself by what you've known or limit your potential by what others say is possible. When the light of opportunity shines, may you recognise it and step boldly into a greater self.

The uncomfortable truth: the average lifespan is about 76 years. Middle age isn't 50 – it's closer to 38. We've been tricked into working until 60, leaving only about 15 years to truly enjoy life. Why spend our best years proving we live, rather than truly living?

Life is meant to be lived fully – being present in every moment.

Too often, we waste time showing others we're alive, without ever truly feeling alive ourselves. It is in presence that life's deepest meaning is found.

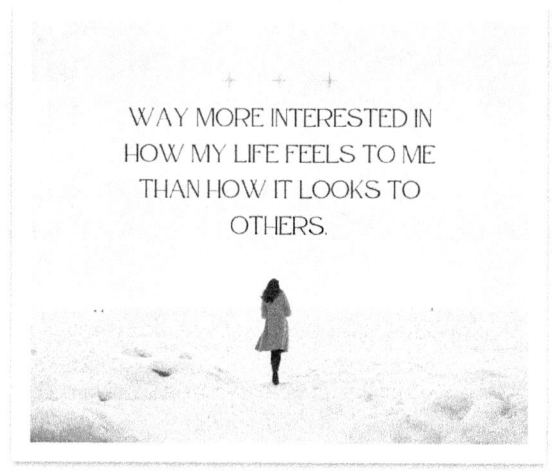

Empathy – You Don't Know What People Are Going Through:

When Did Everything Become Commercial and About Money?

Tim Berners-Lee, a man we should all know about. Please remember his name!

He gifted the world the World Wide Web – not as a product to be sold, but as a shared space for humanity. In 1989, amid the quiet halls of CERN, he sketched a vision of connection, openness, and free exchange. His creation was not an invention to be hoarded or monetised, but an offering – a foundation upon which the world could build, explore, and communicate.

In an age where nearly everything carries a price tag and value is too often measured in dollars and cents, Berners-Lee's example invites us to reconsider the true nature of contribution. What does it mean to create something for society, rather than for profit? When did our world become so consumed by commerce that the idea of a pure, generous gift feels revolutionary?

Berners-Lee's legacy reminds us the human spirit goes beyond accumulation. It calls us back to a world where innovation serves collective good, generosity is its own reward, and the richest currency is the advancement of humanity itself.

Perhaps the real question is not *when* did everything become commercial, but *when* did we forget that some things – like knowledge, connection, and progress – are meant to be freely given.

"Tim Berners-Lee stands as a beacon for that forgotten possibility, urging us to remember that the greatest gifts are those shared without expectation."

– Inspired by *This is Everyone,* **the intimate memoir by Tim Berners-Lee**

Blink and You'll Miss It – The Career Sweet Spot:

Modern careers often resemble a paradoxical race against time – where the finish line is blurry, and the rules are unwritten.

In the early stages, you're dismissed as too young, too green, too raw to be trusted with responsibility. Yet, just as you begin to accumulate wisdom, confidence, and a sense of direction, the narrative shifts: now you're too expensive, too set in your ways, or – worst of all – no longer relevant.

The so-called "sweet spot" of a career is less a stable phase and more a fleeting moment, almost imperceptible in real time.

It challenges our obsession with mastery and success, suggesting instead that fulfilment may not lie in arrival but in the act of becoming – of navigating the tension between not yet and no longer.

The sweet spot, then, is not a destination to reach but a perspective to cultivate: to find meaning, not in perfect timing, but in imperfect growth.

The Emotion Behind Every Purchase:

> Nike sells → Motivation
> Amazon sells → Convenience
> McDonald's sells → Happiness
> Disney sells → Memories
> Apple sell → Status
> Ferrari sells → Status.
>
> Sell the emotion, not the service.

What all these companies have in common is their ability to tap into deep, universal emotions that people crave.

We're not just buying their products; we're buying a piece of something larger – something that makes us feel better, more alive, and feel more in control of our lives.

Emotions are at the heart of what we truly want – and what companies expertly sell. Whether it's motivation, convenience, happiness, memories, trends, or status, it's these intangible feelings that we long for, and companies have learned how to harness them perfectly.

So next time you make a purchase, pause and ask yourself:

"What am I really buying?"

Be Careful What You Chase:

> Once you get a Michael Kors bag, you won't ever want a Target bag again.
>
> But once you get a Chanel bag, the Michael Kors bag becomes unattractive to you.
>
> And once you get a Birkin? You will never settle for a Chanel again.
>
> I'm not talking about bags...

Be Mindful of Your Advice:

"You can't tell a man to pick himself up from the bootstraps when he's bootless."

– Martin Luther King

This simple yet profound statement cuts to the heart of compassion and understanding. It reminds us that true help requires seeing the whole person – not just their potential, but also their present reality. Advice, no matter how well-intentioned, can fall flat or even wound if it fails to meet someone where they truly are.

Consider the story of Rishi Sunak, then UK Prime Minister, who met a homeless man at a shelter. In an attempt to engage, he asked if the man was in business, offering a chance at a job in finance. The man's quiet reply – that he would welcome such a job but first needed to get through Christmas – speaks volumes.

In that moment, the man's words revealed a struggle far deeper than employment: the daily fight to survive, to find warmth, food, and hope amidst hardship. The offer, while kind-hearted, felt distant from the man's immediate reality. It was a reminder that before grand solutions can be embraced, basic needs must be met, and the human spirit must be acknowledged.

This story challenges us to reflect: How often do we offer advice or solutions without truly listening? How often do we impose our ideas of what someone "should" do without understanding the weight they carry?

To give advice with true wisdom is to first listen with empathy and humility. It is to recognise the silent battles others fight – battles invisible beneath their smiles or struggles. It is to honour their pain, their fears, and their present needs before urging them toward the future.

In a world quick to judge and quick to fix, let us slow down. Let us remember that the timing and context of our words matter deeply. And above all, let us give advice not from a place of superiority, but from a place of shared humanity.

Before You Criticise Others:

"Whenever you are about to find fault with someone, ask yourself the following question:

What fault of mine most nearly resembles the one I am about to criticise?"

– Marcus Aurelias

Suffering – The Way of the World:

Suffering is an inevitable part of life – something no one can escape.

Yet, we often make it worse by telling ourselves stories to avoid facing the truth. We create imaginary problems and unnecessary suffering, all in the name of chasing happiness or success.

People suffer not only from failure but also from success.

- We struggle with not having enough money, and then suffer the stress of having too much.
- We crave the CEO job, only to find that the weight of responsibility is far heavier than expected.
- We long for more friends, then feel overwhelmed by too many superficial connections.

The truth is, suffering isn't just about what we lack – it's an intrinsic part of human existence. The more we chase, the more we gain, and the more we have to lose. The more we achieve, the more we must manage and protect.

Suffering is not something to avoid, but something to understand and embrace. It's not a curse, but a natural condition of life. By accepting suffering as part of our journey, we learn to navigate it with grace.

True peace comes from understanding it, not escaping it.

The Art of Asking the Right Question:

When faced with a challenge, our instinct is often to fix what's visible – make things faster, more efficient, cheaper, etc.

In the case of train travel: make them faster, lay new tracks, invest billions to save minutes. High Speed 2 (HS2) is a prime example: a multi-billion-pound infrastructure project designed to reduce travel time between UK cities.

But are we asking the right question?

Rory Sutherland, Vice Chairman of Ogilvy UK and behavioural science advocate, offers a powerful reframing:

"It's rarely a lack of engineering that limits innovation. It's a lack of imagination in defining the problem."

Rather than asking how to make the train faster, ask: how we might spend the billions to make the journey more enjoyable, more convenient, and more memorable?

The Eurostar didn't just compete on speed – it transformed the experience. With comfortable seating, central city arrivals, and even the option of wine mid-journey, the Eurostar made time on board feel like part of the trip, not time lost.

When we ask better questions, we discover better answers – often cheaper, more sustainable, and far more human. Perhaps the true innovation isn't in making trains fly down tracks, but in making passengers wish the journey lasted just a little longer.

 – Inspired by Rory Sutherland TED Talk

Who Do Smart People Learn From?:

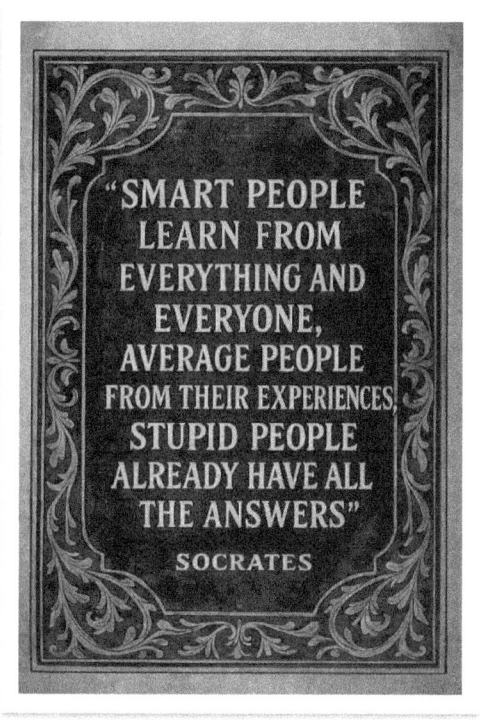

What Needs to Change in Society:

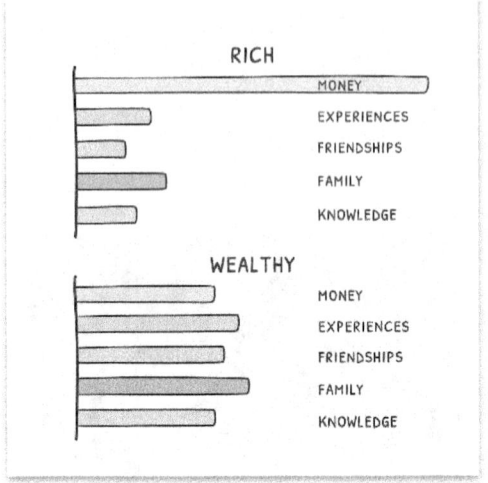

Too many people today value their lives in monetary terms, and make choices based on fear, not love:

They no longer value nor live with **integrity**.

They no longer value nor live with **morals**.

They no longer value nor prioritise **health**.

They no longer value nor invest in **long-term community**.

They no longer value nor respect **difference**.

Be the person **who does.**

The "Emperor(s)" in the Executive Suite:

Over the past 30 years, working with more than 25 of the world's largest corporations, I've observed exceptional leaders alongside cautionary tales. The contrast has been striking, offering invaluable lessons on both what to do and what not to do. One of the most enduring lessons is this: in today's corporate world, the modern emperor still wears no clothes – but now the applause is louder, and the silence more deafening.

In the gleaming boardrooms of glass towers, where titles are tall and language polished to a sheen, a strange quiet often prevails. Not the silence of agreement, nor the pause of deep thought – but the silence of fear. The modern emperor walks exposed, yet the court applauds his robes.

We live in an age where candour and sharing a tangential point of view is risky and caution is currency. Senior leaders – those entrusted with governance, vision, and truth – too often become spectators to power, bound not by principle but by the quiet panic of self-preservation (clearly visible in their eyes). To challenge the CEO or even their inner circle is to flirt with exile – from influence, from income, from the warm glow of relevance.

And so a theatre unfolds. Power parades unchecked, draped in illusions spun from praise and optimism, while those closest to the throne nod with studied enthusiasm. Bad news in the C-suite is like the proverbial hot potato – no one wants to hold it, they look for a "fall guy" and the messenger fears getting shot.

Courage has become a rare currency in corporate halls, especially with personal ambition at stake. They celebrate culture in town halls, keynote speeches and strategy decks, but in real meetings, they defer. The ancient child who once cried out "But he has no clothes!" would now be ushered quietly out by HR.

The real test of a leader – and of the culture they shape – is whether the truth can be spoken without punishment.

Realities of Corporate Life:

In the world of corporate life, there is a subtle but profound truth that often goes unspoken: no matter your title, your tenure, or the friendships you cultivate, the workplace remains a place of work – not family.

This reality can feel harsh, even cold, but embracing it is a form of clarity – an antidote to the illusions that cloud professional life. Colleagues may share laughter, lunches, and even moments of vulnerability, yet beneath the surface flows an undercurrent of roles, goals, and expectations. Their loyalty is often to the company's mission or their own advancement, not to you personally.

The philosopher Epictetus reminds us:

"Make the best use of what is in your power, and take the rest as it happens."

In the corporate arena, what is within your power is your effort, your integrity, your professionalism. What lies beyond your control are the shifting alliances, the office politics, and the transient nature of workplace relationships.

To conflate colleagues with friends or family is to risk confusion and disappointment. It is to mistake a shared environment for unconditional belonging. And yet, understanding this does not mean rejecting kindness or camaraderie – it means honouring boundaries, protecting your inner self, and navigating wisely.

Success – Understanding the Context of the Game:

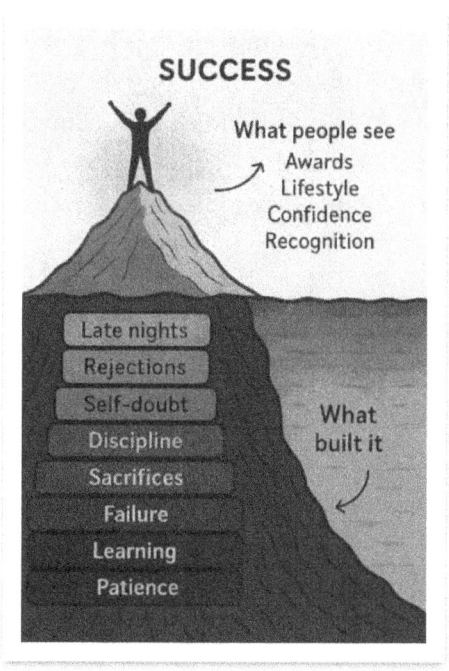

The Corporate Mirror of the School Drop-off:

At the edge of every school day, just outside the entrance where learning begins and ends, a quieter theatre unfolds – not among the children, but among the parents. Here, in this space of asphalt and chatter, something almost comically profound takes root. But beneath this simple surface of goodbyes and greetings, the grown-ups perform a complex dance that mirrors the very corporate politics their children will need to navigate in decades to come.

In this arena, cliques form as naturally as condensation on a winter window. There are the mothers with matching yoga mats and iced coffees, the quiet observers whose smiles stretch a little too wide, the fathers standing apart with their phones out – trying to look busy and posturing casual disinterest. There are gatekeepers and newcomers, whispering alliances, and the occasional display of social currency, a holiday plan LOUDLY shared, always within earshot ("Maldives again for Christmas darling?"). The children may wear uniforms, but the parents, curiously, seem to wear masks.

And in those moments, driven by insecurity, the lines between charm and calculation blur, you find the heart of it – **where some call you "darling and hun"** with syrupy voices whilst their eyes scan the crowd to ensure they are not missing out on better prospects.

What's more intriguing, some parents use the school gate not just as a social checkpoint, but as a calculated platform to elevate their own status – "status games." They target specific individuals – those with influence, appeal, or perceived social capital – with almost corporate precision.

The intrigue of life is not just in watching the charades at play – but in realising that even here, beneath the playground smiles and pick-up-line pleasantries, the boardroom never really sleeps.

When Work Becomes Identity:

In the relentless pursuit of work, many lose sight of who they truly are. They labour not from passion or purpose but to prove their worth, to show the world a carefully crafted image of success.

This endless race of one-upmanship is a silent tragedy, for every achievement demands a price – often paid in moments of missed presence, forgotten joy, and neglected self.

As Sadhguru observes:

> *"Today people just go on working, working and working. Not because they are creating something fantastic, but simply because they have to work, otherwise they don't know what to do with themselves."*

This speaks to a deeper malaise: work becomes an identity, a shield against confronting the emptiness beneath.

True fulfilment arises not from ceaseless toil but from remembering that our value is not measured by output, but by being – by reconnecting with the essence beyond the endless grind.

To live well is to know when to work, yes – but also when to pause, to reflect, and to rediscover the self that no amount of labour can replace.

The Price of Love and Costs of Illusion:

In today's Instagram-driven world, where "over-the-top" is glamourised and price is mistaken for purpose, the engagement ring and the cost of a wedding has become less about love and more about social signaling. Yet, the evolved person sees through such illusions, and chooses meaning over superficiality.

Epictetus reminds us:

> *"Wealth consists not in having great possessions, but in having few wants."*

I met with a wedding photographer recently who told me that in the past they would charge a deposit of 20-25% upfront for wedding shoots then take 25% on day before the wedding day and then the remaining balance on handing over the wedding albums and cd drives. Things now had changed such that they now take all the money ahead of the wedding day, as a significant number of brides and grooms do not want to see the pictures after returning from the honeymoon. What a sad state of affairs.

If love must be proven with precious stones, destination weddings, elaborate gifts, and ostentatious honeymoons, then it is already shaky in its foundation.

The modern pursuit of lavish activities as a prelude to lifelong commitment invites a tragic irony: the more one invests in the ornament, the less one seems to invest in the character of the bond itself.

And so it is in marriage – when craving spectacle or validation outweighs quiet companionship, longevity withers. True love, like virtue, is austere. It does not parade; it perseveres.

Thus, let us not measure commitment by karats but by character. Let the wedding activities be modest and let the virtue of the union speak for itself. For a marriage that endures is forged not in diamonds, but in the quiet of shared purpose.

The World Is Made Up of Two Types of People:

"There are two types of people in the world – the ones seeking knowledge and the ones that want to believe."

– Frederich Nietzsche

Nietzsche explored the dichotomy of human curiosity and belief, revealing how our desire for understanding shapes our interactions with the world.

He contrasts those who question, and those who accept, challenging us to examine which path we follow.

This philosophical insight encourages a deeper engagement with life's mysteries, urging us to question, learn, and grow rather than accept at face value.

Nietzsche's insight challenges us to reflect:

Are we asking the hard questions?

Or are we settling for inherited answers?

Such a call to intellectual curiosity fosters a more examined and meaningful existence.

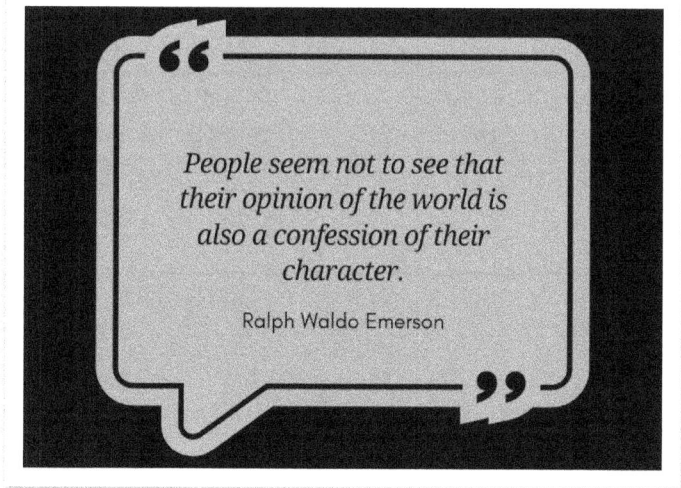

Success at What Cost:

"Your family is broken but you're going to fix the world."

– Naval Ravikant

It's a haunting line – not because it lacks truth, but because it exposes the very tension so many of us quietly carry. The ambition to make a mark on the world... while the people closest to us fall through the cracks.

We celebrate those who chase greatness, who build empires, who speak on stages and solve global problems. But what's the cost of becoming someone to the world if you are no longer someone to the people who once called you by your first name, not your title?

The philosopher in us asks: *What is success, if it breeds distance? What is legacy, if it's built on neglect?* You can be admired by millions, and still not truly *known* by your child. You can solve systemic issues, and still fail to show up with presence at the dinner table.

Maybe that's what Naval was pointing to – the absurdity of a culture that reveres public victories and overlooks private bankruptcies. We chase meaning "out there" while avoiding the mess "in here." But the truth is, no amount of applause will fill the silence of a home you no longer recognise.

Nature of Success:

Success is not a fixed destination but a continual journey – a path defined by the mindset we carry. Those who embrace growth, who see every challenge as an opportunity to learn and evolve, are the ones who move forward with steady steps.

Success is found in the act of persistence itself: in choosing to rise again after each fall, and in the quiet resolve to keep going when the way is unclear. It is less about reaching a final goal and more about becoming someone who refuses to stand still.

To succeed is to live as a river flows – always moving, always adapting, carving new paths through the landscape of life.

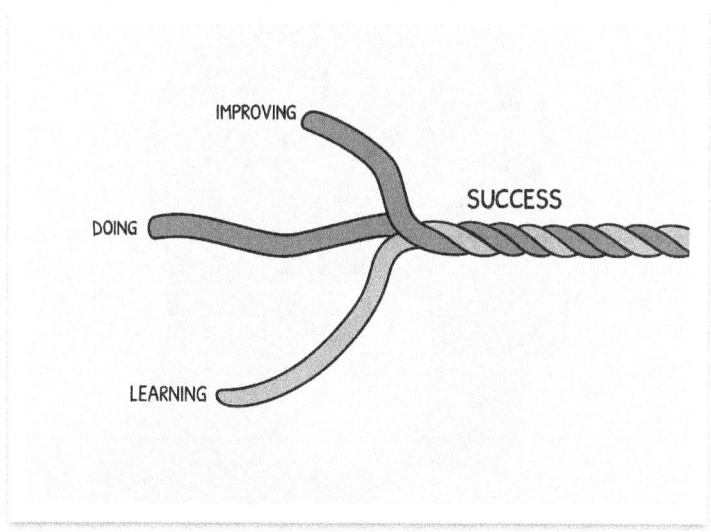

Common Lies We Tell Ourselves:

We often believe stories that hold us back:

"If I had more time, I'd do it."

"If I had that, my life would be better."

"If I tell them this, they'll change."

"I can't live without this."

"I know what I'm doing."

These thoughts are not truths but excuses born from fear and hope. Real freedom comes when we see beyond these lies and face life as it is – imperfect, uncertain, and always changing.

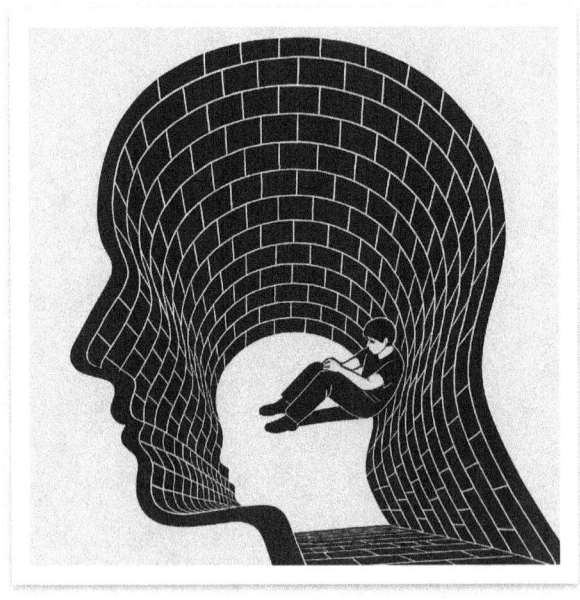

The Downside of Success:

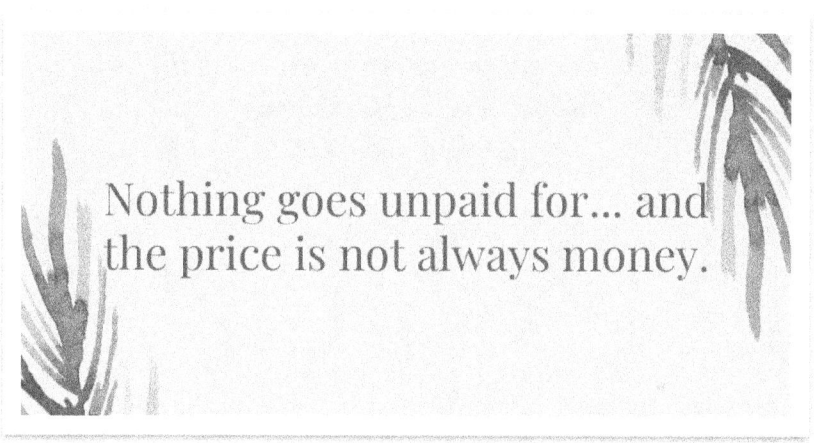

Rising Above the Game:

*"To me, the real winners are the ones who step out of the game entirely,
who don't even play the game,
who rise above it."*

– Naval Ravikant

Functional Depression – Living a Life Behind a Smile:

There is a quiet suffering that few speak of – a shadow cast not by outward signs, but by the silent struggles within. Functional depression is the paradox of a life lived behind a smile, a facade of motion masking a stillness of the soul.

You move through your days fulfilling roles – the worker, friend, parent, caretaker – weaving your responsibilities with care. Yet beneath this surface, the mind can become a restless sea, with waves of exhaustion and despair crashing in silence.

You find yourself running endlessly on the proverbial hamster wheel, caught in a cycle of duties and distractions that never seem to pause or lead anywhere new. The worst part is that nobody knows – this quiet, internal battle remains invisible, unshared.

To acknowledge this hidden reality is to recognise that beneath every smile may lie a story untold – a call for understanding, a plea for presence. It invites us to look beyond appearances and to hold space for the unseen battles others quietly endure.

And perhaps the deepest act of courage is to find a way off that wheel – to pause, to breathe, and to reclaim a life where presence and peace, not endless motion, become the true measures of our days.

Relaxation for Successful People:

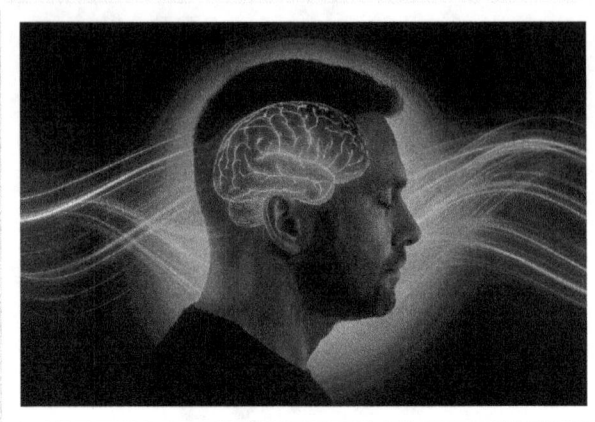

"Competitive people need a flow state with low stakes which allows them to fully relax and switch off."

For successful, driven individuals – those often labelled "alpha" – the greatest paradox is learning to relax.

Accustomed to goal-setting, optimisation, and relentless progress, their minds naturally seek purpose in every activity. Yet true relaxation, the kind that soothes the nervous system and renews the spirit, cannot be achieved through the same metrics that define their success. It must be utterly unproductive, wholly unmeasured, and intrinsically pleasurable.

The irony is that for the most disciplined people, the deepest rest requires surrender: to a flow state without stakes, to a moment that doesn't lead anywhere, to an experience that isn't about becoming better.

Activities like gym workouts, which are seemingly recreational, quickly become arenas for competition – even if only against oneself. In this way, relaxation becomes another battlefield.

The true challenge, then, is not stepping away from work, but stepping away from the very mindset that made them successful in the first place.

Success Without Soul Is Failure:

Success: The fast way is the slow way. And the slow way is the *only* way.

"No great thing is created suddenly."

– Epictetus

Big things take time. Whether it's mastering a skill, building a career, or growing as a person – nothing worth having happens overnight. Instead of rushing, enjoy the process. Focus on the small steps, stay consistent, and trust that good things will come with patience and effort. It's all about the journey, not the sprint.

Anything that's worthwhile takes time and often some discomfort and pain. You need to decide what you are prepared to work at and suffer for. Another way to describe this – success requires consistency of thought and action. To achieve this, you need to ensure you desire the outcome sufficiently and you enjoy the journey to some extent. These positives outweigh any potential pain associated with this.

The one other thing you need to be mindful of is many people are driven by insecurity – by the fear of not succeeding in the eyes of others. That's not ambition. That's avoidance. You are running away from, as opposed to running towards, something deeper and bigger. Succeeding in fake ambition will feel hollow. Chase happiness and contentment, not hollowness.

> In the quiet hours of reflection, do you ever wonder:
>
> Is the person you've become the one you chose to be, or merely the one the world demanded?
>
> And if a piece of your soul was sacrificed to fit in, did you kill it willingly… or did you never notice it slipping away?

Stop Worrying – It's All Immaterial in the Long Term:

Eventually, everyone is forgotten. In just a few generations, no one will remember your name, your struggles, your achievements, and not even your failures.

Whatever feels so important right now will disappear completely.

So, why spend your precious time taking everything so seriously? Why worry about what others think? Why stress over small problems? Why care about mistakes that no one will remember?

Think about it. You're living a temporary life on a tiny planet in an endless universe. Your biggest disasters and most embarrassing moments won't even register in the grand scheme of things.

Instead of creating more problems for yourself, go find some joy. Instead of overthinking, go experience something new. Instead of worrying about your reputation, go make some memories worth having.

Life is too short and too temporary to spend it stressed and serious. Your problems aren't as big as they feel. Your mistakes aren't as important as you think.

Let go of the heaviness. Find reasons to laugh. Create moments of happiness. Make peace with imperfection. No one will remember anyway, so you might as well enjoy the ride.

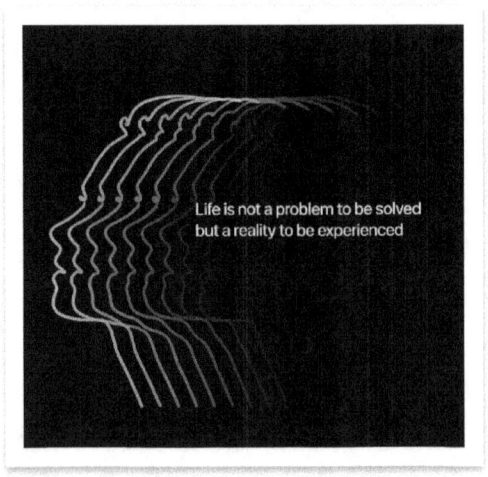

The Fragility of Trust:

"The problem with trust is that first you have to give it away, so that you can take it back if broken."

Trust is a delicate offering – a gift extended without guarantee, a leap into vulnerability. To trust is to open the door of the heart, inviting another in with faith that they will honour the sacred space within.

Yet this gift carries inherent risk. Trust, once fractured, is like shattered glass – its pieces still present but forever altered, reflecting light differently, never quite whole again.

Most only come to understand trust's true value in the wake of its breach, when the ease of faith gives way to caution, and the heart learns to tread more carefully. But it is in the very act of giving trust – imperfect, unguarded – that we affirm our capacity for connection, for hope, for healing.

To withhold trust is to close oneself off from the possibility of authentic relationship, while to give it is to embrace the uncertainty of human imperfection.

Thus, trust remains a paradox: it is fragile and yet essential, vulnerable and yet transformative. It demands courage to give, wisdom to guard, and grace to rebuild when broken.

When Morality Becomes Personal:

"Morality is simply the attitude we adopt towards people we personally dislike."

– Oscar Wilde

See people as they are – don't add a moral lens to someone's behaviour just because you dislike them.

It's amazing how the inverse is also true – people turn a blind eye to close friends who do or say things that don't align with their values.

Competition vs. Collaboration:

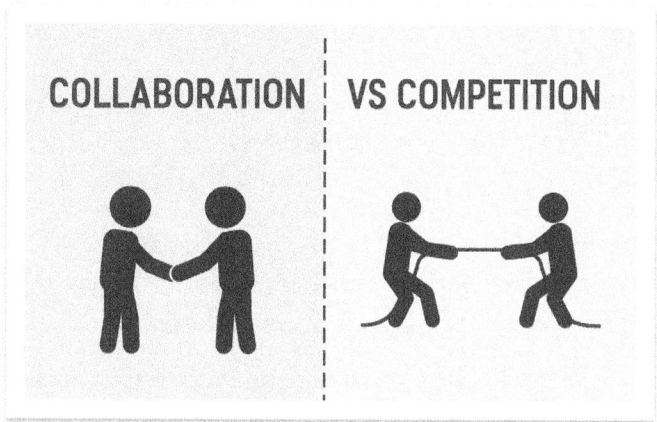

Competition is fierce at the bottom because that's where most people operate – fighting for scraps, seeking validation, and focusing on outdoing others instead of outgrowing themselves.

The scarcity mindset keeps them trapped, thinking success is a limited resource. But real power doesn't come from tearing others down; it comes from building something greater. Those who rise above the noise understand that true success isn't about winning small battles – it's about creating lasting impact.

At the top, the game changes. The most successful people don't waste energy on petty rivalries; they align with others who share their vision.

They recognise that collaboration accelerates success in ways competition never could. They exchange ideas, leverage each other's strengths, and build networks that expand opportunities. Instead of hoarding knowledge, they share it, knowing that true abundance is created through connection, not isolation.

The mindset shifts from "How can I beat them?" to "How can we win together?"

If you want to reach the top, stop thinking like the crowd at the bottom. Let go of ego-driven competition and start building powerful alliances.

The real winners don't fight for table scraps – they build the table.

Surround yourself with people who challenge, inspire, and push you forward. Success isn't a solo mission; it's a collective effort. Play the long game, collaborate with the best, and watch how quickly you elevate to new levels.

Curiosity – The Key to Inner Doors:

"The questions you ask yourself can open doors you didn't even know were there."

Life's growth is not always marked by visible milestones or grand achievements – it often unfolds quietly, in the private realm of thought.

The deepest transformation begins not with answers, but with questions.

The moment you ask yourself something honest – *Who am I, really? What do I want? Why does this matter to me?* – you begin to shift.

Questions are not signs of uncertainty; they are invitations. They are the keys that open hidden doors within the soul, revealing parts of you long buried or never before seen.

Growth is not about knowing everything, but about being brave enough to ask and humble enough to listen.

Sometimes, a single, sincere question can reroute the entire direction of your life. It's not clarity we must chase, but curiosity – because within the right question lies the path to becoming who we were always meant to be.

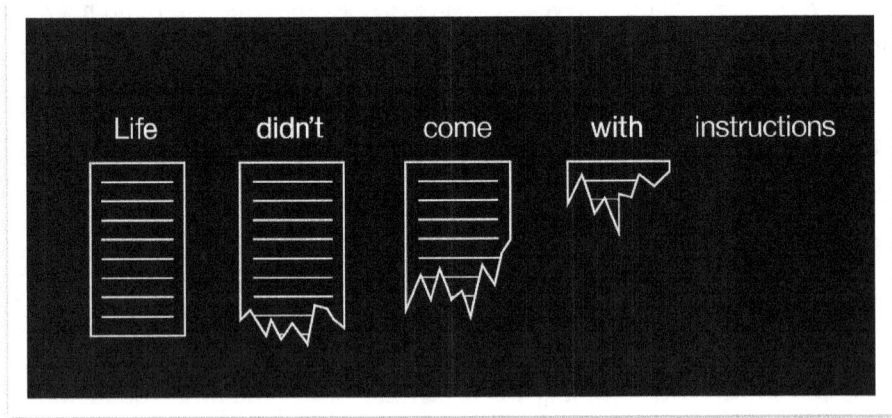

What Is Normal to You… May Not Be Normal to Others:

Be Careful Not to Chase Illusions:

"The hardest thing of all is to find a black cat in a dark room, especially if there is no cat."

– Confucius

People often waste time and effort looking for meaning, answers, or solutions where there are none. The black cat represents an illusion – something people believe is there but isn't real.

It can be applied to many aspects of life-such as overanalysing situations, chasing illusions, or believing in false ideas. Sometimes, people become obsessed with finding hidden truths or solving problems that aren't real, leading to frustration and confusion.

Guard your energy.

Not every question needs an answer.

Not every silence needs interpretation.

And sometimes, the wisest thing you can do… is leave the dark room.

The Price of Privilege:

The 2019 college admissions scandal, **"Operation Varsity Blues,"** exposed widespread bribery and fraud used by wealthy families to secure spots for their children at elite universities, including Yale, Stanford, and USC. The scheme involved fake athletic profiles, cheating on entrance exams, and large bribes to coaches and university officials.

At its core, the scandal revealed the **moral misconduct of the rich**, who exploited their wealth for unfair advantages in a system already biased in their favour.

"It is not the man who has too little, but the man who craves more, that is poor."

– Seneca

The sad thing is that I see similar instances of privilege and entitlement at grassroots level. Examples include, parents involved in local soccer and cricket clubs, not out of genuine commitment to the club's wellbeing, but to influence decisions for their own children or friends' children. It's a sorry state of affairs, but something that only individuals can hold themselves accountable for.

Until we each reflect on and take responsibility for the ways we tilt the playing field, fairness will remain an illusion.

Status Games – The Game of Insecurity:

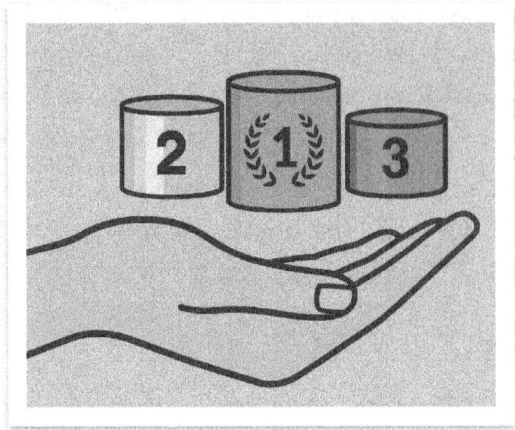

In *The Status Game*, Will Storr explores how much of human behaviour is rooted in our pursuit of status – a deeply embedded drive that shapes our relationships, ambitions, and even our moral beliefs.

At the core of his argument is a powerful insight: **insecurity often fuels the quest for status**. People seek recognition not merely out of pride, but from a need to quiet inner doubts about their worth.

As Storr writes,

> *"Status games are driven not by arrogance, but by insecurity. We play to prove to ourselves that we matter."*

These games can offer meaning and identity, but they also extract a price: envy, burnout, division.

The deeper challenge is learning to discern when our status ambitions truly serve our growth – and when they start to consume us. In the words of Naval Ravikant:

> *"The only way to win is not to play."*

Sometimes, the real power lies in opting out.

When Enough is Never Enough:

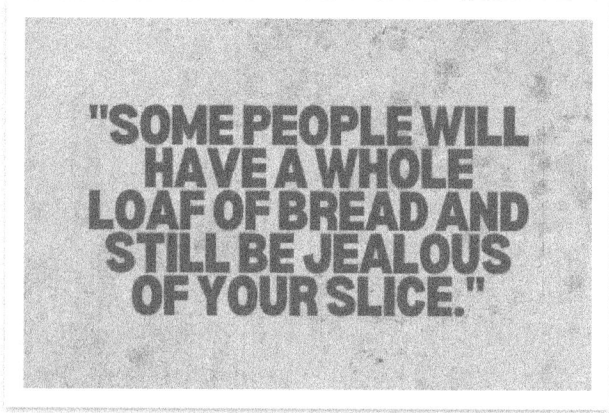

Jealousy and greed are shadows that linger even in the brightest rooms. I have seen it with my own eyes – people who seem to have it all, wealth, success, admiration – yet their eyes flicker with envy at the sight of your small slice of life. It is a painful truth, one I have felt deeply and witnessed time and again among those who, by all measures, should be content.

What is it that fuels this restless hunger? Why does the mind grasp for more when it already holds so much? Jealousy is not about what others truly have; it is about what they represent – a reflection of something missing inside, a quiet emptiness no possession can fill. Greed is the insatiable voice that whispers, *"Not enough, never enough,"* regardless of how full the cup may be.

This reality is deeply personal to me because I have walked through it – watching faces I once admired twist in quiet bitterness, feeling the sting of being envied despite my own struggles. It reveals a profound lesson: abundance is not measured in what we have, but in what we truly appreciate. It is a reminder that the richest souls I have known are those who celebrate another's joy without shrinking their own, who find peace in gratitude rather than power in possession.

Because in the end, no one's slice diminishes another's – except in the narrow mind of envy. And it is in choosing love over jealousy that we finally become whole.

The New Normal – A Quiet Tragedy:

What we call "normal" today is a subtle surrender – a collective quiet desperation masked as routine.

Normal is medicated minds, numbing the sharp edges of pain.

Normal is the heavy fog of work stress that clings to our every waking hour.

Normal is the invisible chains of expectation shaping our worth.

Normal is debt weighing down dreams, a silent burden many bear alone.

Normal is emotions untamed and ignored, storming beneath a calm surface.

Normal is the restless ache of FOMO – chasing a life we no longer recognise.

Normal is 7 hours lost into screens, disconnected from the world and ourselves.

Normal is needing holidays not for joy, but for escape and repair.

Normal is ignoring our body's signals, running until there's nothing left.

Normal is losing track of time, living on autopilot without presence or purpose.

Normal is choosing how others see us over how we truly feel.

Normal is living for the approval of others, while our own voice fades away.

Normal is relinquishing control of our days, letting life slip through our grasp.

Normal is chasing money, measuring value in currency instead of meaning.

But ask yourself, is this truly normal?

Does this silent erosion of our souls not scare you?

And worse still – we are teaching our children to follow this path, to accept this as their fate.

This is not normal. This is a quiet surrender.

To reclaim life, we must first awaken from the fog, and remember what it means to truly live.

Because the greatest tragedy is not a life lost – but a life never truly lived.

The Puzzle of Life:

Life is a vast, intricate puzzle, and every person we meet holds a piece of that mystery. No encounter is random; no moment wasted. Each connection, however brief, offers insight, a hint of understanding, and a chance to glimpse the bigger picture.

Too often, we move through our days guarded, cautious, waiting for certainty before we act. We pass strangers, miss chances for connection, and cling to the familiar edges of our puzzle, afraid to explore the unknown.

Timothy Leary reminds us:

> *"Trust your instincts, do the unexpected."*

That leap – the surprising conversation in an elevator, the smile exchanged in a coffee shop line – can unlock new parts of ourselves we never knew existed. It's in those moments of vulnerability and curiosity that the puzzle begins to shift, revealing patterns once invisible.

The puzzle of life asks us to be brave: to reach out when it's easier to retreat, to listen when it's simpler to ignore, to step forward when instincts say stay safe. Because on the other side of that courage lies growth, connection, and meaning.

So, trust that every person you meet carries a piece meant for you. And remember, the puzzle only makes sense when you're willing to see beyond the edges of your own piece – and hold the pieces of others with care.

Part V: Wealth, Freedom & Long-Term Thinking

Themes: Money, Meaning, Simplicity, Legacy

A Life Worth Looking Back On:

Ultimately, it doesn't matter what you do in life. What matters is that you can one day look back and remind yourself:

You were young once!

And you had some truly great times.

Time – The Here and Now:

In 30 or 40 years, many will look back and realise they would give up vast amounts of wealth just to reclaim the health and vitality they have today. Yet, in the present moment, we often take for granted the precious gift of being well – body and mind intact, the simple joys of movement, breath, and clarity.

We forget that time is fragile and fleeting; tomorrow is never guaranteed to hold the same blessings as today. The here and now is all we truly possess – the foundation upon which every future moment depends.

To live fully is to honour the present, to cherish the health and peace we have now before it becomes a memory. True wisdom lies in embracing this moment deeply, for time is not just a measurement, but a sacred space where life unfolds.

The Paradox of Presence and Loss:

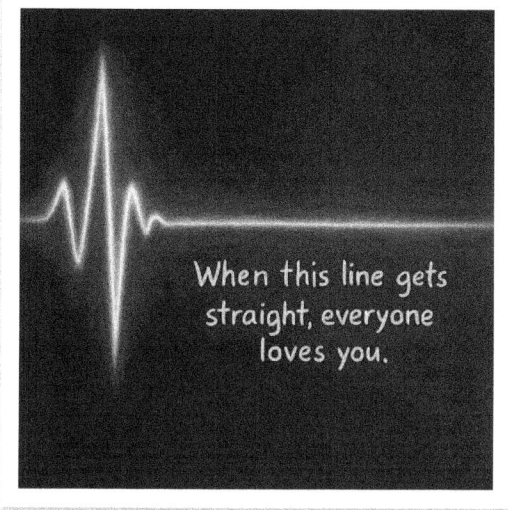

Life is strange in the way it teaches us the value of love – often too late.

When someone is gone, the silence they leave behind echoes louder than their presence ever did. Suddenly, the moments we took for granted become sacred, and the words left unspoken weigh heavy on the heart.

People show love more openly after loss because grief strips away pride and fear, revealing the raw truth of our feelings. It's as if absence sharpens the clarity of what truly mattered, and in trying to honour what was lost, we finally express the depth of love we never had the courage – or time – to show when it could have made a difference.

As Marcus Aurelius once said,

"Do not act as if you were going to live ten thousand years. Death hangs over you. While you live, while it is in your power, be good."

The Meaning Can Only Be Found in Doing the Thing:

The best parenting advice I've ever received was quietly profound:

"Enjoy that time, that day, that season, that year with them – you and they will never be given that second-grade year again."

And I've had to remind myself of this constantly – especially as a parent who's chosen to place their children in high-achieving schools, where excellence is the baseline and comparison is baked into the culture. The pressure to succeed can become invisible, yet overwhelming. It's easy to start treating every activity, every subject, every choice as a stepping stone to some greater achievement. But that mindset, even when well-intended, robs them of something sacred: the right to simply be a child.

Reshma and I have had to step back and let them pick things they enjoy – even if they don't shine at them, even if it won't land them on stage or on a podium. I've had to remind myself that they are not here to fulfil unfulfilled dreams or build a future before they've even built memories. They are here to play, explore, be silly, and sometimes do things badly – for no other reason than joy.

High-performing environments can make it hard to let go of the scoreboard, but childhood is not a competition. Not everything needs to be measured, polished, or perfected. Sometimes, the bravest thing we can do as parents is to shield them from the wrong environment, the wrong circle of influence, "the race" and teach them how to wander and just be.

They will be adults all too soon. The world will push them to achieve, produce, and compete.

But for now, it's on us to make space for wonder, for rest, for unstructured joy. That is the childhood they deserve. And that is the gift we must fight to give them.

The Power of Awe:

The Stoic philosopher Marcus Aurelius once said:

> *"Dwell on the beauty of life. Watch the stars, and see yourself running with them."*

Awe has a way of stopping us in our tracks and reminding us just how beautiful and mysterious life really is. It gives us goosebumps, lifts our spirits, and even changes us physically – it slows our heart rate, calms our mind, and makes us feel more connected to something greater than ourselves.

This is awe. It's not about big, dramatic moments. Sometimes, the smallest things carry the deepest wonder – a warm beam of sunlight, the shape of a tree, your first cold breath on a winter morning, or the comforting smell of coffee.

These little moments, often called *glimmers*, gently pull us back to the present. They remind us that life is not something to rush through, but something to feel.

You don't need to climb a mountain to feel awe. Just notice what's around you.

Let those small, beautiful moments open your heart. That's how awe works – it humbles us, heals us, and quietly brings us back to ourselves.

The True Meaning of Financial Freedom:

Financial Freedom = Passive Income > Burn Rate

Financial freedom means having enough passive income – money earned with little ongoing effort – that it exceeds your burn rate, or the amount you spend to live each month.

When this balance is achieved, you no longer rely solely on active work to cover your expenses, giving you the power to choose how you spend your time.

It's not just about wealth; it's about reclaiming freedom, reducing stress, and creating space to live life on your own terms.

Passive income becomes the quiet engine that supports your dreams, allowing you to focus on what truly matters without the constant pressure of paycheque to paycheque.

Work – Are You Climbing the Right Mountain:

Imagine getting to the top of a mountain and realising it wasn't the one you wanted to climb.

You spent years working your way up the career ladder, chasing titles and trying to hit month end, quarter-end and year-end targets. And after 5, 10, or 15 years of driving yourself and your team you finally arrive at where you thought you wanted to be, but something does not feel right. It's not pride. It's emptiness.

We live in a world that glorifies being busy, promotions, monetary success and not least job titles.

The real question is not "How successful are you?" but "Are you headed where you intended, and does it fulfil you in the right way?"

Because it is far better to be climbing slowly up the right mountain than fast up the wrong mountain. Truth is: you can be successful in the eyes of others and still feel lost and empty.

If you feel like this… you're in the wrong role or career… Take a pause!

There is no shame in pivoting in a considered way to something that gives you that excitement and fulfilment on a daily basis again.

The Texture of a Winning Life:

There's a moment in every life – quiet, often unexpected – when a piece of advice doesn't just land, it lodges itself deep within the architecture of who you are. For me, it was this:

"Exceptional people play to win, they don't play NOT to lose!"

At first glance, it sounds like ambition. But beneath the surface, it's about something far more profound: mindset, courage, and the way we relate to risk, fear, and purpose.

Average people, through no fault of their own, are often shaped by caution. They make moves designed to protect what they already have. Their efforts are defensive – measured by what they might avoid, not what they might become.

Exceptional people live differently. They do not merely seek to survive the game – they seek to *transform* it. They lean into discomfort, take the shot even when they might miss, and speak up when silence would be safer. Their lives are not dictated by the desire to avoid loss, but by the will to create meaning.

These are the kinds of moments that make up the true texture of life – not the titles, not the trophies, but the awakenings. The small, soul-shifting reminders that how we choose to live – boldly or timidly, fully or halfway – is the difference between being merely alive and being truly human.

Success Is a Direct Reflection of Effort:

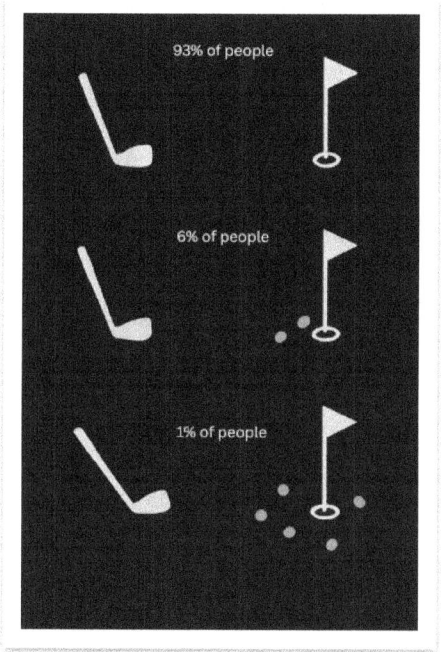

Success is not an accident – it is a direct reflection of effort. To achieve results in the top 1%, one must be willing to put in what 99% will not: consistent, disciplined, and often unseen work. Talent may open the door, but effort keeps it open. In every field, those who rise above do so not by chance, but by choice – the choice to work harder, longer, and with greater intention. As Kobe Bryant once said:

"Great things come from hard work and perseverance. No excuses."

The more effort you apply, the more opportunities seem to appear – what many call "luck" is often just the visible result of invisible hours.

Words That Change Lives:

"Read books, read stories, share stories. You may never know which thought or fact may resonate with you and change the course of your life."

– Avdhoot Sherkar

I'm hoping that the words in this book touch many.

Limits on Wealth – What Money Cannot Buy:

Money is a tool – a means to acquire many things – but it cannot buy the most essential treasures of the human experience. True fulfilment lies beyond material wealth, in realms that touch the depths of our being and the vastness of existence.

Consider these qualities that elude monetary exchange:

- Soul-mission alignment: living in harmony with one's deepest purpose.
- Inner peace: a calm that arises not from circumstances, but from within.
- Wisdom beyond time: insights that transcend the fleeting moments of our lives.
- Integrity in silence: moral courage that remains steadfast even when unspoken.
- DNA activation: awakening the dormant potential encoded within us.
- True spiritual sovereignty: owning one's path with freedom and authenticity.
- Vibrational discernment: sensing truth beyond words or appearances.
- Purpose-driven living: acting in alignment with a meaningful cause.
- Telepathic trust: a silent knowing between souls.
- Sacred relationships: bonds that nourish and elevate beyond the superficial.

These are the currencies of the soul, forged not in gold or silver, but in presence, awareness, and grace.

Best Time to Do Anything:

"Best time to plant a tree was 30 years ago, the second-best time is now."

– Chinese proverb

Making Change Happen:

"Nothing changes if nothing changes."

– Common Saying

Change is the bridge between desire and reality, yet many stand at its edge, unwilling to cross.

People often wish for better outcomes while clinging tightly to familiar routines, hoping transformation will come without discomfort. But growth demands disruption. To create a new reality, one must release the old, embrace uncertainty, and become an active force in the process.

Change does not happen to us – it happens through us. Only by owning the drivers of change – our choices, our mindset, our actions – can we shape the lives we truly want. Comfort may feel safe, but it is often the cage that keeps us from becoming who we're meant to be.

Modern Day Laziness – Being Busy:

"Beware the barrenness of a busy life."

– Socrates

Modern laziness is not idleness; it's a frantic rush that leaves no room for thought or truth. We pack our days with endless tasks – so-called "responsibilities" – that push aside moments meant for presence and purpose.

We claim to seek meaning, yet the noise of daily demands – caring for others, maintaining routines, fulfilling obligations – engulfs us. These burdens can feel like chains, but are they truly responsibilities, or distractions in disguise?

Too often, our lives live us, swept along by relentless momentum. True freedom, however, lies in seizing control – choosing consciously what deserves our focus and what does not.

In the stillness beyond busyness, we face ourselves and find the measure by which we will judge our lives. The art of living is to step back, see clearly, and live intentionally – not by default.

As Epictetus teaches:

"It's not what happens to you, but how you react to it that matters."

Though we cannot control everything that fills our days, we hold the power to choose how we respond – and in that choice, true strength is found.

Wealth Is Freedom, Not Acquisition:

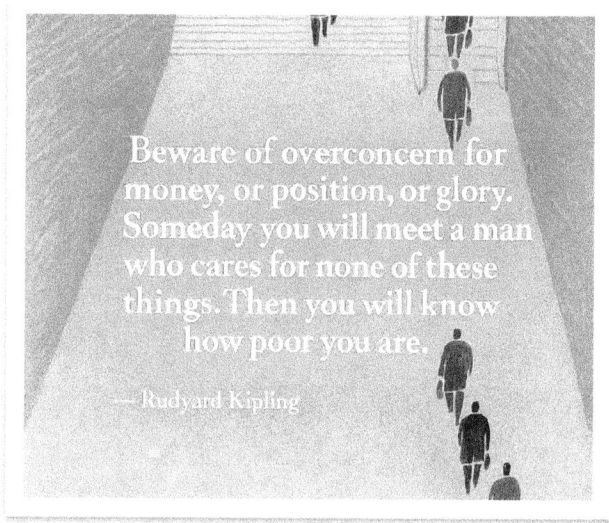

True wealth is not measured by the size of your bank account or the status symbols you collect: it is your net assets minus your ego. When you reach a place where extra money no longer dictates how you spend your time, who you spend it with, or what you aim for, you have stepped into real wealth. You are wealthy not because of what you have, but because of what you no longer need.

Wealth shows itself the moment you can say no. When you can deny future earnings because you already have enough – that is true freedom. Yet, few ever arrive here. For most, "enough" is a moving target, forever chasing a horizon that keeps retreating. The goalposts shift, and the hunger grows, fuelled by ego and fear.

Remember this: The point of making money is not to buy anything and everything. The point is to buy your freedom – the freedom that ensures no one else can ever buy you. True wealth is found not in endless acquisition but in the power to choose your own path without compromise.

The Paycheque Cage:

> **THE GREATEST PRISON HAS NO BARS – JUST A PAYCHECK, A ROUTINE, AND WEEKENDS OFF.**

Money Is a Means, Freedom Is the Goal:

Money itself is not the destination – it's simply a tool on the journey. What we truly seek is freedom: freedom from the weight of society's judgements, freedom from the noise of others' opinions. Freedom from the constraints of the 9-to-5 grind, where every minute is dictated by someone else's clock.

Freedom from manipulation, from invisible forces trying to shape who we are or what we become. Freedom to choose the people we surround ourselves with, to curate a circle that lifts us rather than drains us. Freedom to spend our time and energy on what truly matters, without apology or compromise.

Money opens doors, but freedom is what lets us walk through them on our own terms. And that – freedom – is the real goal.

> **Ever met a rich person who's miserable? That's what happens when you win the wrong game. Money is great but without health, deep relationships, and time to enjoy life, it's an empty victory. Success isn't just numbers, it's a life well-lived.**

Money, Work, and Influence – The Pareto Effect:

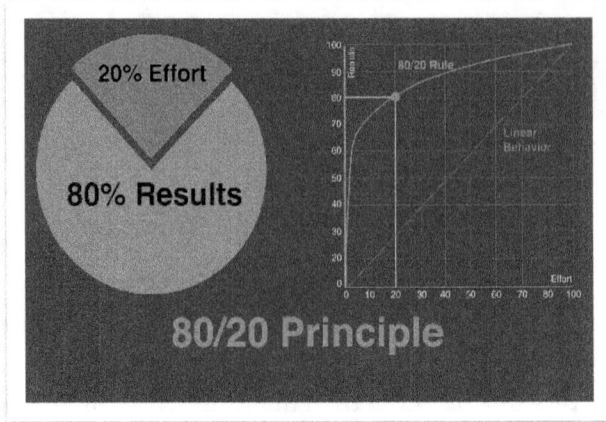

Not everything in life follows a neat, bell-shaped curve. While many things – like height or weight – fall into what we call a normal distribution, much of our world operates by a different rule: the Pareto Distribution.

This principle reveals that a small portion of causes often leads to a large portion of effects. It's the reality behind the saying that 20% of employees do 80% of the work, or that 20% of customers bring in 80% of the revenue.

Take wealth, for example: roughly 20% of people own 80% of the wealth.

Why?

Because money breeds opportunity, and opportunity breeds more money – a self-reinforcing cycle that concentrates resources. This pattern challenges our assumptions of fairness and equality but also offers a powerful lens to understand where focus and effort truly matter.

The power of Pareto Distribution lies in its call to action: to identify and invest in the vital few – the critical 20% – rather than dispersing energy evenly across the many. Understanding this imbalance allows us to work smarter, not harder, and to recognise the hidden dynamics shaping success, influence, and impact in our lives and societies.

Money Magnifies Who You Truly Are:

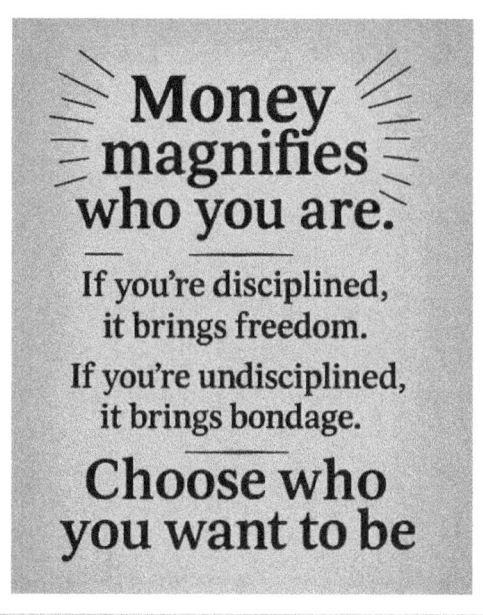

The Quiet Grace of the Working Life:

This resonates deeply with Reshma and me, as we both come from working-class and business families. We must never forget that we work to provide – for ourselves, our families, and the continuity of life. In a world flooded with messages about "following your passion" and "living your truth," it's easy to overlook that, for many, work is not about identity or fulfilment but survival. Yet, there is dignity in that truth.

There is profound nobility in the working person – the one who rises not out of love for the job, but out of responsibility. The person who works 35-40 hours a week, not to chase a dream, but to ensure a home, a meal, and a future. While society often celebrates those who find joy in their careers, we should offer equal, if not greater, honour to those who show resilience, quiet perseverance, and the courage to show up, regardless of inspiration.

Life's essence isn't only in extraordinary pursuits but in the **small victories of the ordinary**: a dinner after a long shift, a peaceful walk home, laughter on a Sunday. These are not lesser lives; they are deeply human. Marcus Aurelius wrote, *"Do not hanker after what you do not have. Instead, fix your attentions on the finest and best that you have."* This is the discipline of gratitude, of seeing clearly.

To live well isn't always to live loudly. Sometimes, it's to move through the world with integrity, providing what's needed and finding meaning in what is, rather than chasing what might be. In honouring the quiet grace of the working life, we reaffirm that every life lived with purpose, no matter how unseen, is worth admiring.

Currency of Life:

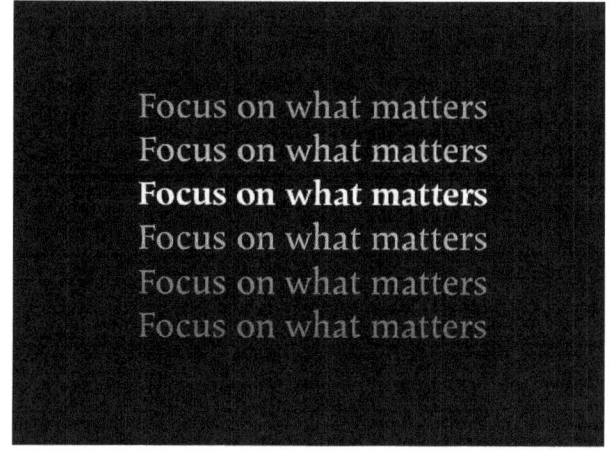

The true currency of life is neither money nor time – it is attention.

Money can be earned and lost, time flows whether we notice it or not, but attention is the one resource we spend moment by moment, shaping the very quality of our existence.

Where we place our attention is where our life unfolds. In the quiet exchange of glances, in the depth of a conversation, in the way we watch the light fall through a window – this is the wealth of being alive.

To give full attention is to say, *"This matters."* And yet, in a world that demands our focus in fragments, it is a radical act to offer it fully.

The richness of life lies not in how much we do, but in how deeply we live what we do – how present we are to each emotion, each connection, each breath.

If we learn to spend our attention wisely, we will find that we have always been wealthier than we knew.

The Red Car Theory – Where Attention Goes Reality Follows:

The "Red Car Theory" suggests a simple, almost whimsical observation: once you decide to buy a red car, or someone mentions one to you, you start seeing red cars everywhere. But this theory isn't just about automobiles; it's about attention, awareness, and the quiet but profound power of focus which is important not just in your personal life but in your daily life at work. What we attune our minds to, we begin to perceive more readily in the world around us – not because the world has changed, but because *we* have.

Philosophically, this mirrors a deeper truth about consciousness: our experience of life is not solely dictated by what *is*, but by what we are *looking for*.

If we train our eyes toward pain, disappointment, and failure, the world will appear saturated with these things. But if, instead, we deliberately choose to notice moments of kindness, beauty, and connection – like red cars on a busy road – we begin to see them multiply. Not because they weren't there before, but because they were hidden beneath the noise of neglect.

In doing so, the good things in life – once rare and fleeting – begin to appear more frequently. A smile from a stranger. The light between trees. The quiet resilience in your own breath. All there, waiting to be seen.

Greed – When is Enough Enough?:

This story is neither about gold nor is it about a boat!

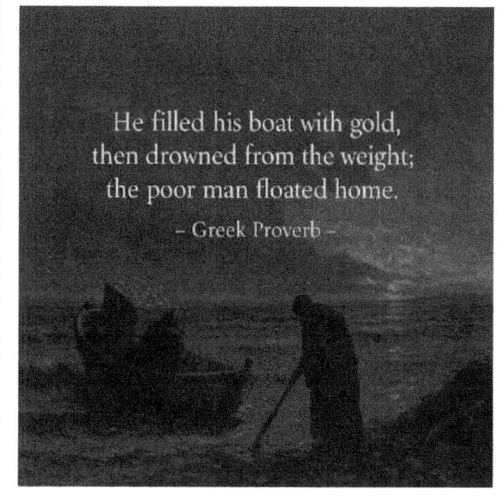

No Such Thing as a Free Lunch:

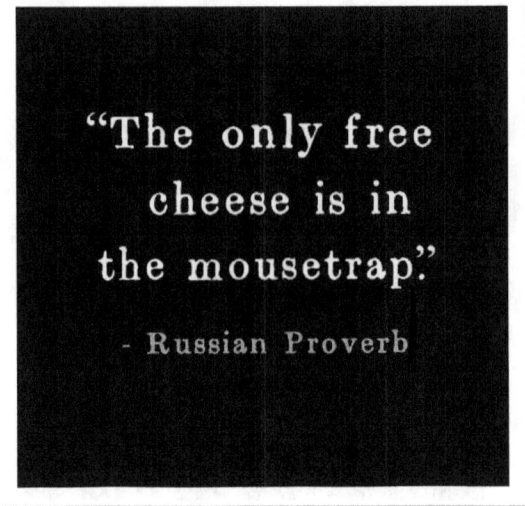

Health – The Most Important Lesson in Life:

"The person who recovers from open heart surgery best is the one that doesn't need it in the first place."

The single most important lesson in life!

Investing for the Future Takes Patience:

The Power of Choosing How We See the World:

"There is a kind of sadness that comes from knowing too much, from seeing the world as it truly is. It is the sadness of understanding that life is not a grand adventure, but a series of small, insignificant moments, that love is not a fairy tale, but a fragile, fleeting emotion, that happiness is not a permanent state, but a rare, fleeting glimpse of something we can never hold onto. And in that understanding, there is a profound loneliness, a sense of being cut off from the world, from other people, from oneself."

– attributed to Virginia Woolf (1882-1941)

The Greatest Freedom:

"Our greatest freedom is the freedom to choose our attitude."

– Victor E. Frankl

Following Your Passions:

> "Creation is lifework, creation is how you spend your life, you cannot divide life and the creation, it's impossible. Shut your ears, close your ears, don't use your brain, use your heart, your soul."
>
> — Yohji Yamamoto

The Power of Embracing "Enough":

True power lies not in the endless pursuit of more, but in the deep knowing that what you have is enough. To desire less is not to lack ambition, but to awaken to the fullness already present within and around you.

When we stop chasing after the next thing – the next achievement, possession, or validation – we begin to see clearly. We recognise that the hunger for "more" often blinds us to the richness of the moment, the abundance woven into the fabric of our lives.

Contentment is not complacency; it is wisdom. It is the quiet strength to rest in gratitude, to embrace sufficiency, and to free ourselves from the chains of endless longing.

In this knowing, we discover freedom: freedom from dissatisfaction, from comparison, and from the ceaseless noise of desire. The power of not wanting more is the power to be present, whole, and at peace with what already is.

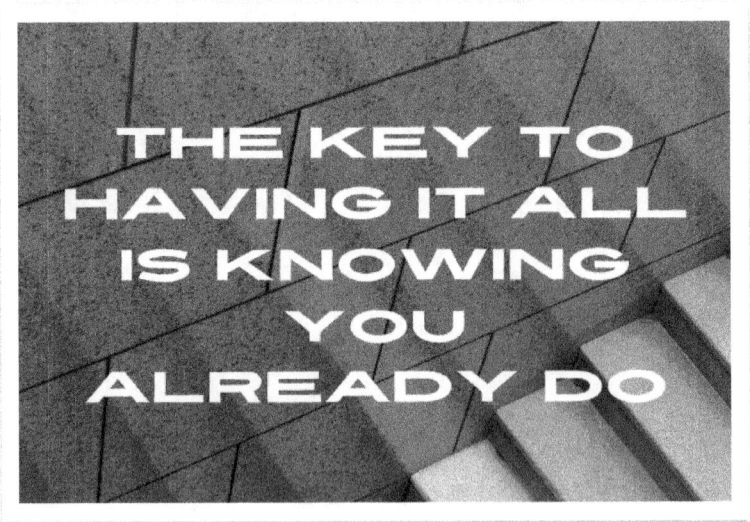

Without Health You Have Nothing:

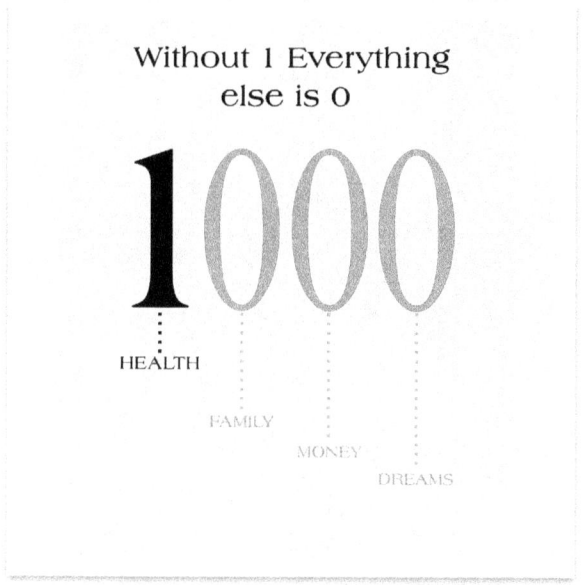

Every Genius Has Its Own Path:

> Everybody is a genius. But if you judge a fish by its ability to climb a tree, it will live its whole life believing that it is stupid.
>
> — Albert Einstein

Part VI: Meaning, Spirit & Inner Strength

Themes: Purpose, Spiritual Growth, Emotional Intelligence

Understanding Life – John Lennon's Experience:

> When I was 5 years old, my mother always told me that happiness was the key to life. When I went to school, they asked me what I wanted to be when I grew up. I wrote down 'happy.' They told me I didn't understand the assignment, and I told them they didn't understand life.
>
> – JOHN LENNON

Our Ancestors – We Walk On Their Strength:

Title: The *Highest Bidder* portrait hangs in Oprah's home as a daily reminder of the suffering, strength, and resilience of our forefathers.

A mother and child, captured in a moment of unimaginable loss, stand on an auction block in 1906 – sold to the highest bidder, not as humans, but as property. It is a portrait that carries the weight of millions. During the 18th century alone, over 6.5 million souls were ripped from their homelands and forced across oceans, destined for a life of brutal labour on plantations from Virginia to Georgia.

But we must not forget. Not the names, not the faces, not the pain that echoes through generations.

My own history holds exile too – my parents, forced to flee Uganda, stripped of home and safety, compelled to build from nothing in a world that gave them no welcome. Their story, like so many others, is not one of victimhood, but of survival. Of quiet resilience.

We walk on ground laid by those who endured. We inherit both the burden and the strength of their memory. To forget them is to dishonour everything we now stand upon...

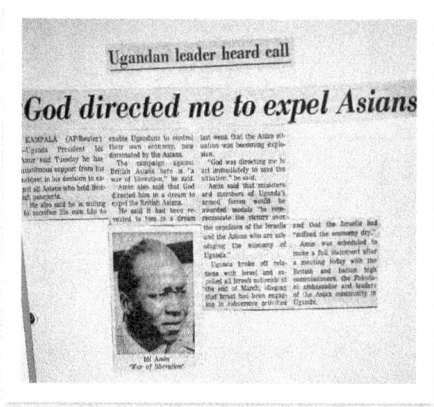

The Power Within – Choosing Your Story:

"If you think someone has ruined your life; you are correct – it's you!"

– Friedrich Nietzsche

Nietzsche's words cut deep because they remind us that the true power over our experience lies within ourselves. Blame is easy to cast outward, but growth demands we turn inward, to face our own role in the stories we tell ourselves.

Yoga offers a beautiful path for this inward journey – not just as a practice of the body, but as a practice of mind and spirit. Through *santosha*, we learn to find contentment in the present, embracing what is rather than what isn't. It softens the harsh edges of disappointment and anchors us in gratitude, even when life's waves crash hard.

Then there is *svadhyaya* – self-study – which invites us to watch our thoughts and emotions with curiosity instead of judgement. The more we reflect, the more we recognise the patterns that trap us, and the clearer our choices become. In this daily discipline, we reclaim the power to shape our reactions, to grow wiser, calmer, and more compassionate with ourselves.

Ultimately, the power of self-reflection shows us that the life we feel ruined is the same life we have the strength to rebuild.

The Pulse of the Crowd, The Meaning of Life:

The privilege of living in North London with proximity to Wembley Stadium and other London venues has allowed us to engage with hundreds of concerts and sporting events over the years. I've often tried to quantify the pull of live events versus the comfort of enjoying them from home.

There is a rare and transcendent beauty in live concerts and sporting events – not merely in the music or the game itself, but in the collective human spirit that gathers around them. In these moments, something ancient stirs: the longing to belong, the need to be part of a tribe, to feel the pulse of others beating in rhythm with our own.

We are not meant to be solitary islands. We are wired to gather, to share in joy, in heartbreak, in suspense and release. When I go to these events, I find myself watching the faces around me more than the stage or the field. There's a certain glow in people's expressions, in their singing, in their chants – not manufactured happiness, but something deeper. They are lost in the moment, swept away by the tide of sound, of movement, of unity. For a brief while, no one is worried about tomorrow. In the chant of a crowd or the silence before a note drops, we are all just *here* – breathing the same air, feeling the same emotion, creating physiological memories!

This, I believe, is the meaning of life. Not in grand answers or distant philosophies, but in these small, electric moments of togetherness – where joy becomes contagious, and we remember that we are not alone and part of a broader collective.

In these shared experiences, we don't just witness life – we *live* it.

The Sacred Truths of Being Human:

There is a quiet, ancient wisdom in the rules handed down through time – guidelines not for control, but for awakening.

You are given a body, not by choice, but as a vessel through which to experience life.

You are here to learn, and life itself is your teacher.

Every challenge, every heartbreak, every detour is not a mistake, but a lesson in disguise. And until you learn what it came to teach, it will return in different forms, gently – or sometimes forcefully – asking you to pay attention.

Growth is not a destination; it is a lifelong unfolding.

You will long for "there," believing it holds more peace, more joy, more meaning – but everything you seek is already *here*.

Others in your life are not strangers to your soul; they reflect what lives within you – your fears, your beauty, your unfinished stories. Your life is yours to shape, not according to others' expectations, but from the truth that lies deep within you. And yes, you will forget. You will lose your way. But the remarkable part is: you can remember. At any moment, you can return to yourself, to your inner knowing, and begin again.

That is the sacred, simple truth of being human.

From Craving to Gratitude – The Journey of Valuing:

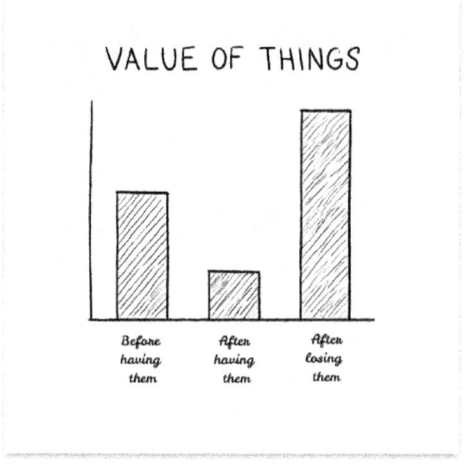

There is a curious rhythm to the way we value the things in our lives – be they friendships, possessions, or fleeting moments – that reveals much about human nature. Before we have them, they gleam with promise and possibility, painted in the colours of our desires and hopes. In that anticipation, they hold immense power; the mind elevates them, building castles of meaning around what is not yet ours. But once possession is secured, the glow often fades. The extraordinary becomes ordinary, and what was once dazzling slips quietly into the background of everyday life. Familiarity dulls the edge of wonder, and we begin to take for granted what we once craved.

Yet, the deepest lesson comes only when these things are lost. Suddenly, their value returns with a fierce intensity, often magnified by regret and longing.

This cycle of valuation teaches us that value is not fixed; it is a living thing, shaped by absence and presence, by memory and expectation. It calls us to be more mindful – to cherish before loss, to remain present in possession, and to hold gratitude for what once was.

In this way, the ebb and flow of value becomes a quiet teacher of appreciation, reminding us that the treasures of life are not in the having, but in the conscious awareness of their meaning to us.

Karma as Choice, Not Judgement:

Karma is often misunderstood as a system of punishment or reward, a cosmic scoreboard tallying our deeds. But at its essence, karma is neither judgement nor favour – it is simply the natural consequence of the choices we make. Every action, thought, and intention sets into motion a chain of cause and effect, rippling outward in ways both seen and unseen.

This unfolding is impartial, neither cruel nor kind; it simply *is*.

To live wisely is to embrace responsibility for these consequences, not with fear, but with awareness. The true challenge lies not in controlling outcomes, but in understanding the subtle web of cause and effect – especially the unintended consequences that often catch us unaware.

Mindfulness in choice becomes the compass that guides us through the unseen paths of karma.

By recognising that every moment is a seed planted, we learn to sow with care. Karma is not a burden to dread, but a mirror reflecting the quality of our intentions.

It calls us to act with clarity, compassion, and integrity – knowing that what we give is what we become.

The Strength of a Gentle Soul:

> she has a wild spirit,
> but a soft heart,
> and such a sweet soul

The strength of a gentle soul emphasises that gentleness isn't weakness – it's moral clarity and quiet strength. This is dedicated to Reshma, my wife. This perfectly articulates who she is.

Some souls are so gentle and pure, they witness every detail – the hurt in someone's smile, the lie behind a laugh, the silence after a betrayal – and still, they remain confused. Not because they lack awareness, but because their hearts can't make sense of cruelty, dishonesty, or indifference. They understand the world… but not why people choose to wound it.

"You will meet bad people, but your duty is not to be like them."

– Marcus Aurelius, Meditations

This echoes the idea that even when beautiful souls see and feel everything – including injustice or cruelty – their role is not to understand or mirror it, but to remain steadfast in their own virtue.

Beautiful souls need to be celebrated as they have so much to offer and the fact that they never need to treat people that way.

Definition of Real Beauty:

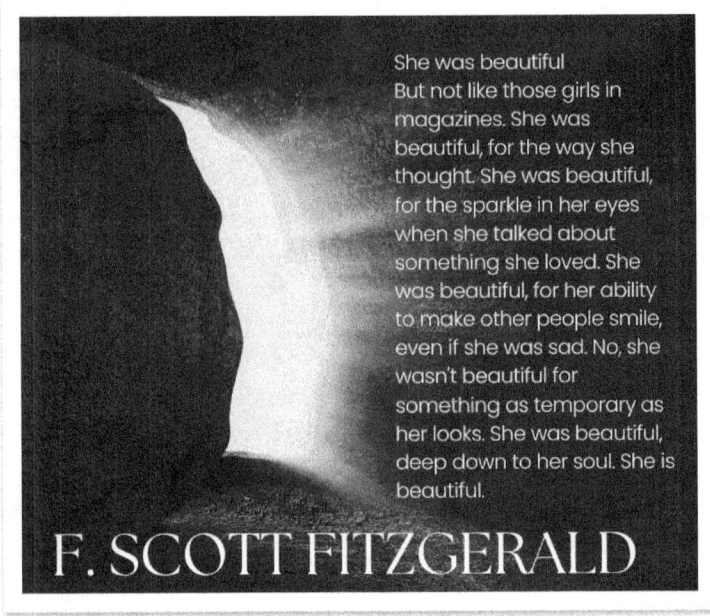

Be the Change – The Quiet Power of Small Acts:

"Waste no more time arguing about what a good man should be. Be one."

– Marcus Aurelius

Those who truly seek to change the world do not wait for permission or perfect conditions – they simply begin.

They carry within them an unshakeable belief: that every single life holds infinite value. They find profound meaning in the smallest acts – a smile, a kind word, a moment of connection.

They understand that transformation is not born from grand gestures, but from the quiet persistence of tending to one wound, feeding one hungry soul, nurturing one curious mind.

Their aim is not to overturn the entire world overnight but to plant seeds of change, however modest, trusting that these small acts, multiplied over time, ripple outward to reshape the fabric of life.

True impact lives in the steady courage to act where you stand, knowing that the smallest light can break the deepest darkness.

No Man Walks in the Same River Twice:

The Quiet Power of Forgiveness:

"Forgiving people in silence, and never speaking to them again a form of self-care!"

Forgiveness is often seen as a grand gesture – an open conversation, a heartfelt apology, a bridge rebuilt. Yet, sometimes the deepest form of forgiveness is silent. To forgive in silence is to release the weight of resentment without reigniting the past or reopening wounds.

This silent forgiveness is not about reconciliation or forgetting; it is a radical act of self-care. It is the choice to free oneself from the chains of anger and bitterness, even if the other remains distant or unchanged.

In forgiving silently, we claim our peace, protect our energy, and affirm that our well-being does not depend on the actions or acknowledgment of others. It is a quiet surrender to the truth that forgiveness is less about them and more about healing ourselves.

True strength lies not in confrontation, but in the grace of letting go – without fanfare, without expectation, simply in the stillness of our own hearts.

The Power of Your Imagination:

Ernest Hemingway captured this best in what's considered his shortest story:

"For sale: baby shoes, never worn."

Six words. A universe of emotions.

Where does this take you?

Joy Without Reason:

Joy is one of life's great equalisers – pure, undiluted, and unburdened by justification.

It needs no grand reason, no noble origin.

It simply is.

Whether it springs from a child's laughter, a quiet moment at the end of a beautiful film, or a windswept day by the sea in Portsmouth, its essence does not change. Joy, in its truest form, is free from hierarchy or judgement.

It does not care for status, wealth, or intellect.

It visits all of us, and when it does, it reminds us what it means to be alive. To feel joy is to be touched by something sacred and fleeting. And sometimes, in our better moments, we become its conduit – we are the reason someone else feels that spark, that lightness, that lift of the heart.

What a privilege that is.

A life devoted to joy – not only in receiving it, but in giving it freely, humbly, without expectation – might be the most meaningful life we can hope to lead.

For in those moments, we are closest to the core of what it means to be human.

The Eulogy We Write Each Day:

How we live is how we are remembered. When the final words are spoken about us, they rarely dwell on job titles or bank balances. Instead, they echo the feelings we inspired, the kindness we extended, and the love we shared.

At life's end, people won't recall the hours we spent at the office or the accolades we amassed. They'll remember the warmth of our presence, the comfort of our words, and the joy we brought into their lives. They'll speak of the times we listened without judgement, stood by them in hardship, and celebrated their successes as if they were our own.

Legacy isn't built on professional achievements; it's woven through every-day acts of compassion and integrity. It's in the laughter we share, the support we offer, and the lives we touch. As Matthew McConaughey reflects,

> *"We're all authoring our eulogies through our daily choices and interactions."*

So, consider this: If you desire to be remembered as someone who uplifted others, start by offering a helping hand today. If you wish to be seen as a beacon of kindness, let your actions reflect that now. Living with intention and compassion ensures that your legacy will be one of love and positive impact.

Live in a way that, when remembered, brings a smile to someone's face and warmth to their heart.

– Inspired by Jimmy Carr in the DOAC podcast.

Strength in Vulnerability and Restraint:

There is a profound strength in silence, in the choice to withhold the full measure of ourselves from those who cannot yet hold it with honour.

"Never defend yourself..."

Epictetus advises, teaching that defending against criticism often gives it more power than it deserves. When someone speaks ill of us, it is not a weakness to stay quiet or to respond with quiet humour:

"He does not know my other faults; else, he would not have mentioned only these."

This response holds within it a wisdom that transcends ego and invites humility.

Weak people hide their flaws behind a mask of strength, flaunting what they think makes them invulnerable. But true wisdom lies elsewhere. Wise people wear their flaws openly, not as shields, but as badges of lived experience and growth. As Brené Brown reminds us,

"Vulnerability sounds like truth and feels like courage. Truth and courage aren't always comfortable, but they're never weaknesses."

To be vulnerable is not to be weak; it is to be authentically human.

"Don't let your ego blind you." This is a call to humility, to seeing beyond the illusions of pride and fear. When we let go of the need to prove ourselves, when we stop defending the fragile self we think others must accept, we step into a deeper, quieter power – one that understands strength is not in showing off, but in knowing when to hold back.

In this restraint, there is freedom. In this humility, there is grace. And in this grace, there is the truest kind of strength.

"Drowning Child" – The Moral Duty to Help:

The "drowning child" thought experiment, proposed by philosopher Peter Singer, argues that distance shouldn't negate our moral obligation to help others when we can do so without great personal cost.

It uses the scenario of a person passing a pond where a child is drowning, highlighting that saving the child requires minimal effort and sacrifice (like getting wet or ruining clothes).

Now, what if that child wasn't right in front of you, but in a neighbouring town, or across the world? Would the distance make your responsibility any less real?

The question of "how far away" becomes irrelevant in this context, as the moral obligation to help remains regardless of physical distance if the ability to help is present and the cost to the rescuer is minimal.

Conclusion:

If you can help someone no matter how far away they are, and with no expectation of reciprocity then we all should.

"Let's not forget that we are human beings."

Self-Confidence – The Irrefutable Definition:

"Giving the world irrefutable evidence with your actions that you are who you say you are!"

– Alex Hormozi

Turning a Mid-Life Into the Pivotal Years:

> Nobody talks about the middle. The part where excitement fades and progress stalls. Where the work feels endless, the wins feel small, and the finish line isn't even in sight. The middle part is where most people quit—not because they couldn't do it, but because they thought it wasn't supposed to feel this way. But this is actually where the growth happens. Push through. One day, this chapter will be the part of the story you're most proud of.

Living Amongst Dreams Made Real:

As we grow older, our perspective shifts. The world no longer feels like a given. We start to see it not as something that simply *is*, but as something *made*. That hotel didn't just appear – someone imagined it, financed it, fought for it. That park was once just an empty lot until a group of people saw something more. That railway, that bridge, that neighbourhood café – they are all monuments to human will.

Only recently have I begun to truly *internalise* how much persistence everything requires. Not just vision, but grit. The daily resolve to keep going when no one's watching, when the result is uncertain.

The world, in many ways, is a living museum of passion projects – each one a quiet triumph of someone refusing to give up.

As Marcus Aurelius wrote:

"You see how few things you have to do to live a fulfilled and reverent life. And you can do this anywhere."

When we look around with reverence – even at the ordinary – we see not just structures, but the spirit that built them. To live in awe is to live awake. It's to recognise the sacred effort in the everyday.

And in that awareness, we begin to feel not just gratitude, but a sense of responsibility – to build something ourselves, however small, that might one day awe someone else.

Beyond Comfort – The Beauty of a Life Well Lived:

A beautiful life is no accident; it is a deliberate creation – a masterpiece shaped by intention and care. Our minds have the power to seek out the light, framing the positives that guide our actions and choices. Yet, this life is not a product of mere reason, but of the heart's wisdom – a feeling that cannot be fully grasped by logic alone.

True beauty in life grows not from ease or comfort, but from embracing discomfort when it serves a greater purpose. It is forged through commitment to what truly matters, even when the path demands struggle. This is the life worth living.

As the waves shape the shore, so too should we make waves in our own existence – never content to be mere spectators. Look back not with regret, but with the certainty that you moved, you stirred, you mattered.

Do not live tethered by the expectations and obligations of others, so much so that you forget your own desires. To live fully is to know yourself deeply and to claim your life as your own.

The Privilege of Everyday Life:

> WHAT A PRIVILEGE IT IS TO EAT WELL ENOUGH TO BE FULL.
> WHAT A PRIVILEGE IT IS TO WAKE UP EVEN WHEN TIRED.
> WHAT A PRIVILEGE IT IS TO BE EXHAUSTED FROM A WORKOUT.
> WHAT A PRIVILEGE IT IS TO HAVE PEOPLE TO MISS.
> WHAT A PRIVILEGE IT IS TO HAVE SO MUCH TO BE GRATEFUL FOR.

Perspective Is a Strange Thing:

We rage at the small stuff – delayed trains, slow baristas, a spilled coffee, like it's a personal attack from the universe. These tiny disruptions set us off, tugging on the thread of our composure until we unravel. We treat them like emergencies. We react, we curse, we lose the day to them.

And yet, when life whispers about the *big things* – we stay silent.

The job that drains our soul.

The dream we once had but now neglect.

The relationships that run on routine instead of realness.

The quiet, creeping sense that we're not really *living* – just existing on autopilot.

These things, the ones that shape the arc of our lives, we push to the background. No panic. No urgency. Just the soft hum of denial.

Why?

Because the small things demand no courage. Just reaction.

But the big things?

They require change. Reflection. Action. The uncomfortable kind – the kind that might upend the fragile life we've settled into.

Perspective & Judgement:

The world is a canvas painted by each person's subjective view. You will never be seen the same way by everyone: no matter what you do, some will admire you, while others may find fault. You'll be a source of inspiration to some, and a burden to others. For some, your strength will be perceived as resilience, while for others, it will come across as fragile. You may be seen as a comforting presence to one, yet "too much" for someone else. Some may feel at ease in your company, while others will feel anxious.

This is the nature of human perception. We all filter our experiences through the lens of our own biases, fears, and desires. You'll be a hero to one and a villain to another. And this will change, as people's perspectives shift with time, experience, and context. But this is not a reflection of you – it's a reflection of their inner world, their lens through which they interpret the world around them.

So, instead of moulding yourself to meet the fluctuating opinions of others, why not focus on understanding the context in which people perceive you? Why not approach the world with curiosity, asking the right questions, and understanding that what others see is often shaped by their own experiences, beliefs, and emotions?

When you live for the approval or judgement of others, you'll always be in flux. But when you live in alignment with your own truth, unshaken by external judgement, you will finally find peace. The world may never agree on who you are, but you might as well live as the person you know you are – true to your heart, unburdened by the weight of others' perspectives.

Birds born in a cage think flying is an illness.

Just because you see the world from your perspective does not make that perspective true for everyone else. Remember this before judging someone.

Life's Direction:

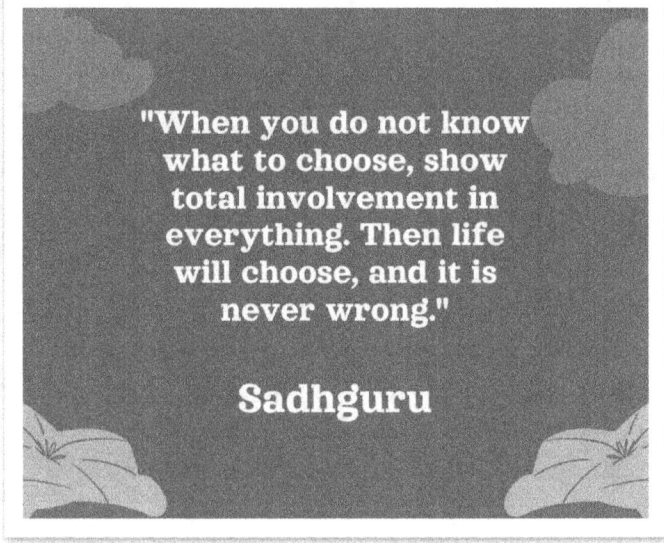

Reframing for Gratitude – The Greatest Privilege:

~~I have to~~

I get to... have breakfast each day with my kids

~~I have to~~

I get to... drop my kids to school each morning

~~I have to~~

I get to... work each day

~~I have to~~

I get to... watch team sports practice for my kids

~~I have to~~

I get to... read the great authors of our time

~~I have to~~

I get to...

Appreciate Your Loved Ones – The Inner Dialogue We Dread Will Come:

"They're late."

"They've never been late."

"Not once, in twenty years."

"They're late."

"Something's wrong…"

"Maybe… maybe they're hurt."

"Maybe something happened."

"Maybe something terrible…"

"Maybe… I'll hear a voice. A voice I don't know. Saying their name, like it's nothing."

"Like it was meant to happen."

"Maybe this is it."

"That moment."

"That moment we all fear, deep down, but never speak of."

"If I call… if I call, it's real."

"If I wait… they're just late"

"… Just late."

The mind, in its quiet terror, teaches us that the weight of love is not in presence, but in the abyss it leaves behind when absence echoes louder than truth

– Inspired by Lohause Sunglasses and Eyewear advertisement

Destiny and the Illusion of Choice:

We often believe that life is a series of decisions, moments where we stand at crossroads, weighing options to shape our future. Yet, perhaps the choices we think define us are not truly ours to make.

As the Oracle in *The Matrix* reminds us:

> *"You're not here to make a choice on a decision, that is already made. You're here to understand why you made that choice."*

This perspective invites a deeper reflection on destiny and self-awareness. Life may unfold along paths already woven into the fabric of our being, and the real journey lies not in the act of choosing, but in understanding the roots of those choices – our desires, fears, and truths that steer us unknowingly.

To live wisely is to move beyond the illusion of free will as mere decision-making and to seek insight into the inner workings of our soul. In comprehending why we have chosen, we uncover the deeper currents of our purpose and destiny.

This is not surrender to fate but an awakening: a call to embrace self-knowledge as the compass guiding us through life's apparent uncertainties.

Time – The Sweetness of Doing Nothing:

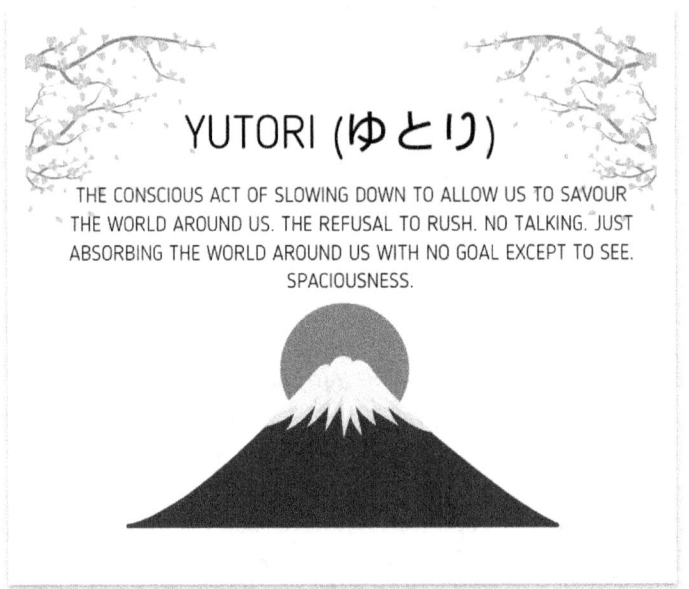

In a world that prizes speed and constant achievement, the ancient practice of *Yutori* – the conscious act of slowing down – offers a radical invitation: to breathe deeply, to savour presence, and to reclaim time as a space for gentle being rather than relentless doing.

It is in this deliberate slowing that we find *Dolce far niente* – the sweet art of doing nothing.

To embrace *Yutori* and *Dolce far niente* is to remember that life is not merely a series of tasks to be completed but a flowing experience to be lived. In the sweetness of doing nothing, we reconnect with ourselves, with others, and with the world in a way that rushing can never allow.

Time Is Your Most Valuable Asset:

Time is the most precious currency we possess – an irreplaceable asset that slips silently through our grasp. Unlike wealth or possessions, it cannot be regained once spent, and its true measure remains a mystery until it is too late.

In the dance of life, our calendars often become arenas of obligation, habit, and ego. We fill our days to prove our worth, to affirm our existence through ceaseless activity. Yet, as the wise remind us:

> *"An overscheduled calendar is not worth living."*

To live fully, we must reclaim time as our own – not as a resource to be endlessly parcelled out at the whims of others. If you find yourself reluctant to attend, reluctant to engage, remember this:

If you don't want to go – don't go.

For those who truly care will respect the boundaries of your time and honour your judgement. The need for their approval is but an illusion.

Your time is sovereign; it demands careful stewardship. The company you keep, and the commitments you accept, are reflections of your inner state. They reveal what you value and how you care for your own well-being.

To invest time wisely is to invest in life itself. Some investments yield richness and growth, while others deplete without return. Your calendar is more than a schedule – it is a mirror, reflecting the quality of your life.

So, hold fast to this truth:

> ***Time is the only currency you cannot create more of, and you never truly know how much remains.***

Choose with care. Guard your space fiercely.

Live not by the dictates of busyness, but by the sovereignty of your own rhythm.

Time – The Invisible Account:

> Time is the only currency you spend without ever knowing your balance. Use it wisely.
>
> – The Universe

4,000 Weeks to Live – Make Them Count:

When What We Do Outshadows What We Become:

We live enslaved by our To-Do lists, endlessly chasing tasks, deadlines, and achievements. Yet, few of us ever pause to write the plans for who we want to become – our To-Be lists.

We are so focused on doing that we neglect being.

But true fulfilment comes not from crossing off actions, but from consciously shaping our character, values, and presence. The question isn't just what will I do today, but who will I choose to be.

Without this awareness, we risk living lives full of busyness but empty of meaning.

Life's Lessons on Anger:

Anger is the fire we kindle within, expecting others to feel its heat.

But in truth, it is we who are burned. To grow angry at another's misstep is to offer ourselves as tribute to their error – to punish our own peace for what lies beyond our control.

The Stoics remind us: what others do is their affair; how we respond is ours. If someone wrongs you, they have acted in accordance with their understanding, their flaws, their ignorance. To let their mistake become your torment is to hand over your mind in chains.

Consider: when you are angry, what is it that you gain? Does your fury correct the wrong? Does it mend the moment? Or does it simply corrode your clarity, obscure your reason, and steal your time?

Anger is a thief in noble disguise – it dresses itself as justice but serves only chaos. Let it pass. Remain still. Respond with reason, or not at all.

"How much more grievous are the consequences of anger than the causes of it."
– Marcus Aurelius

He who masters his anger is greater than he who conquers cities.

The Last Refuge for Creativity – You Will Not See Showers the Same Again:

In an age governed by relentless connectivity, where every pause invites a ping and every silence is filled with scrolls and screens, the mind has become a territory under siege.

Our inner world – once fertile ground for daydreams, insights, and emotional reckoning – now lies cluttered with noise not of our own making. We have traded contemplation for consumption, presence for performance.

Yet, amid this cacophony, there remains one quiet sanctuary: Not a mountaintop in Nepal but a shower in your home!

Here, enveloped by warmth and white noise, the mind finds itself momentarily untethered. There are no notifications, no curated feeds, no digital mirrors reflecting back. Only steam, solitude, and the raw hum of consciousness. In this space, time dilates.

Thoughts meander without purpose, and from this purposelessness springs something rare: creativity unforced, emotions unmasked.

It is in the shower that we rediscover what silence feels like – not just the absence of sound, but the presence of self. With no audience to impress and no agenda to fulfil, the mind remembers how to wander, and in wandering, it often finds something essential: an idea, a memory, a feeling long buried under the weight of busyness.

Here, for a few precious minutes, we are simply ourselves – unfinished, unpolished, and finally, alone.

The Power of Music – It Stirs Emotions:

People don't fully realise the power of music.
It vibrates the air – literally.

We disturb invisible particles in waves,
which enter us and move through us at lightning speed.

These waves of particles conjure up:

- Memories from our childhood,
- Emotion of our first love,
- Pain of our first breakup,
- Our soul being ignited,

All from particles of air vibrating through us.

- It can make us smile,
- It can make us cry,
- It can move our soul at its core.

Music is more than sound.

> *"Music is an emotion encoded to a point in time of our lives."*

No Moment Is Truly Mundane:

This is one of the most touching and devastating books I have ever read. Its message is engraved in me. The opening lines of the book:

"Life changes fast. Life changes in the instant. You sit down to dinner and life as you know it ends."

– Joan Didion, The Year of Magical Thinking

There's no warning. No shift in the light, no tremor in the ground. One moment, the world is whole: the table set, the person you love reaching for the salt, your life wrapped in the comfort of ritual. And the next – it isn't.

Didion's words strike not because they're dramatic, but because they're precise. "*You sit down to dinner and life as you know it ends.*" The horror is not in the extraordinary, but in the fact that there is *nothing extraordinary* at all. The plates and the food are the same. But the world is now irrevocably different.

We often think of catastrophe as something that gives us a sign. But as Didion so plainly writes, life unravels most brutally in the middle of normalcy. Something cruel hides in the way change sneaks in, not with ceremony, but with silence.

What Didion gives us, in her grief, is clarity. A painful illumination that no moment is truly mundane. That behind every ordinary, fragile, sacred evening lies the possibility of rupture – and love, memory, and meaning are all we have when it comes.

Living For the Future Is a Wasted Life:

Living for the future is a wasted life – a truth I've come to feel deep in my bones, even when the world around me insists otherwise. I carry with me two quotes that echo this realisation, grounding me when I drift too far into tomorrow's promise or yesterday's regrets.

> *"He who lives for what is always out of reach. His thirst for survival in the future makes him incapable of living in the present."*
>
> – Chuang Tzu

These words remind me how easy it is to chase a mirage, constantly running toward an ever-moving horizon, missing the breath, the laughter, the simple miracles right here and now. I have known moments when my mind was so tethered to what might come, I was blind to the beauty unfolding around me – the warmth of sunlight on my skin, the quiet comfort of a loved one's presence, the rawness of my own emotions.

And then there's this truth that cuts straight to the heart:

> *"Every man has two lives, and the second life begins when they actually realise they only have one life."*

It is a reckoning, a sudden awakening to the fragile brevity of our time here. It tells me that the first life – often filled with distractions, fears, and endless planning – is just preparation. The second life, that richer, fuller existence, begins when I stop postponing living and start embracing what is, what is real, what is now.

This passage, from denial to presence, is not easy. It requires courage to loosen the grip on the future, to stop bargaining with time and finally surrender to the moment we have. But in that surrender, I find freedom. Freedom to love deeply, to feel fully, to be utterly human. And in this embrace, I am truly alive.

The Future or Are We Already There?

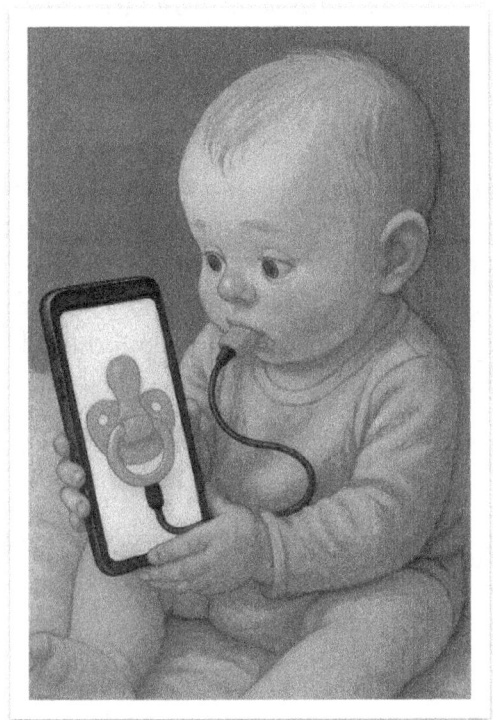

Failure and People's Perception:

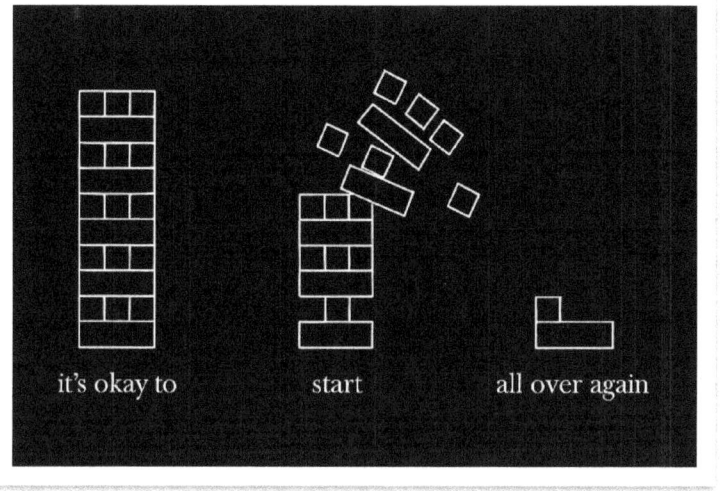

"Failure – you're not afraid of failure but what people will think."

Failure is not truly the fear we wrestle with – rather, it is the fear of how others will judge that failure. The weight of external opinion can shackle our spirit, imprisoning us in a silent struggle where doubt grows louder than courage.

To move forward, we must learn to untether ourselves from the gaze of the crowd. True freedom lies in quieting the noise of judgement, in holding our failures not as marks of shame, but as stepping stones toward growth. Guard your inner world with care: choose who walks beside you, who listens, and who holds your truth.

In this sacred circle, vulnerability can breathe without fear, and failure becomes not a verdict, but a teacher.

Only then can you step boldly into the unknown, unburdened and unashamed, guided by the compass of your own becoming.

Death – An Inspirational Perspective:

A man once asked a monk, "What happens when we die?"

The monk didn't respond with fear, but with peace. Death, he said, isn't an end – it's a return.

We don't disappear; we dissolve back into the infinite. We were never truly separate from it. We *are* the universe, not just a part of it. When we die, we don't vanish – we simply let go of form and return to our true essence.

Life isn't about proving ourselves, passing tests, or obeying a higher power out of fear. It's not about earning our way back. We were never cast out – we came from oneness, whole and complete, and chose to experience life in all its depth.

Like choosing to leave home for an adventure, we stepped into this world to feel joy, sorrow, love, loss, pain, and peace – not because those feelings define us, but because they help us remember who we are.

We don't need to earn our way back to the source. We never left it.

Life's journey – with its mistakes and missteps – isn't meant to shame us, but to guide us. Every choice that feels wrong is a gentle reminder: "This isn't who you are." And through listening, we return to truth.

So why are we here? To experience. To feel. To grow. To remember. And above all, to love.

Because in the end, every path leads home. And the love we give – to others and to ourselves – is what lights the way back.

You are loved.

The Answer is Not in Fulfilling Your Dreams:

Jim Carrey's reflection:

"I wish everyone could get rich and famous and have everything they ever dreamed of, so they can see that it's not the answer."

This quote is simple, but deeply philosophical. At its heart lies a paradox: that the fulfilment of our desires may lead not to satisfaction, but to disillusionment.

When Carrey says that this is "not the answer," he gestures toward a hidden truth – that in chasing the external, we often abandon the internal. And only by reaching the summit of our ambitions can we truly see that the mountain was never the point.

To understand what he meant is to confront a central tension of the human condition: we believe happiness lies in attainment – of wealth, fame, love, success – yet when those things are finally possessed, they often reveal themselves to be hollow or fleeting.

Carrey isn't condemning dreams, nor achievements. Rather, he is urging a deeper kind of wisdom – a shift from believing in dreams as salvation to seeing through them as illusions. It is only once we exhaust the promises of the world that we begin to ask different questions: What remains when the dream is gone? Who am I without the roles I play? What is fulfilment that does not depend on applause or possession?

Thus, his wish is not a cynical curse, but a radical hope – that people might see through the illusions early enough to turn inward, to discover peace, not in success, but in presence; not in acclaim, but in awareness.

We See You, We're Proud of You:

"Just in case no one has reminded you today – *we are so proud of you*.

Not for perfection, not for grand victories, but for the quiet, relentless courage it takes to simply keep going.

We see the battles you've fought in silence, the tears you've wiped away alone, the mornings you've risen when all you wanted was to stay in the dark. You have endured more than most will ever understand, and still, here you are – *showing up*, heart open, spirit intact. That is strength. That is resilience. That is something to be deeply proud of.

We hope you know how deeply worthy you are – how your presence brings light into lives you may not even realise you've touched.

The world is better because you're in it. Your small steps forward are monumental, and your journey – no matter how messy or uncertain – is a testament to your bravery.

You are growing, evolving, healing, and becoming.

And even if today feels heavy, you are not alone.

We see you.

We honour you.

And more than anything, *we are proud of you*.

We hope you are, too."

Part VII: Final Reflections

Themes: Ageing, Closure, Hope

Getting Older Is Strange and Beautiful:

"You don't stop playing because we get old, we get old because we stopped playing."

– George Bernard Shaw

Time moves in paradoxes – some days stretch endlessly, while whole years vanish in a blink.

You wake up one morning and realise your body speaks to you more clearly now – not in words, but in sensations: the longer recovery after a workout, the ache behind a late night, the quiet invitation to slow down.

The mirror shows more *salt* than *pepper*, but it also shows something else: a face that has *lived*, not just existed. A face that has loved, failed, laughed too hard, and made peace with not having to prove anything anymore.

At some point – maybe around forty – you stop trying to keep up and start trying to tune in. Yoga replaces intensity. Stillness starts to feel more powerful than speed. You stop filling your schedule just to feel important. Instead, you raise the bar: on who gets your time, what ideas you feed your mind, and how deeply you show up for your life.

Your inner circle shrinks, but deepens. You crave conversations where the music doesn't drown the meaning. And increasingly, you realise that your *diet* is everything you consume – food, media, energy, and company. It all shapes who you are becoming.

And here's the quiet, unexpected joy: with every year, you feel more like *yourself*. The person in the mirror is no longer a work in progress chasing approval – but a human being in process, grounded and awake.

Seneca once wrote, *"As long as you live, keep learning how to live."* That's what ageing is: the art of refining, releasing, remembering.

So yes, getting older is weird. But it's also a gift – a slow unfolding into clarity, connection, and truth.

A Life Built in Stillness:

I used to think that living life to the fullest meant chasing the big things – quitting my job on a whim, flying to a new country, collecting moments that looked good in photos. But over time, I've learned that the richest kind of life isn't always made of fireworks or key milestones of success.

Sometimes it's made of very quiet, very human moments that ask only for my presence.

Now, I ask myself each day: *What will I thank myself for tomorrow?*

Maybe it's reaching out to someone I've been meaning to call. Maybe it's reading something that shifts my thinking, or simply pausing to sit with my coffee without rushing off. Maybe it's doing something kind without needing recognition. These are the choices that, one by one, build a life I'm proud to live.

I've started to understand that the truest version of "living fully" isn't about adding more – it's about coming home to what's already here. It's learning how to be okay in stillness. How to feel at home in my own skin. How to stop constantly proving, fixing, reaching. To simply let some things be enough.

Maybe, as I've passed my mid-point in life and have a young family, I've come to value the simpler things. I used to chase moments that would wake me up. Now I try to build a life that lets me find peace. A life where the little things hold just as much magic as the big ones. Where the joy comes not from impressing anyone else, but from knowing deep down that I'm exactly where I'm meant to be.

And that, I think, is the most extraordinary life of all.

Living an Unfulfilled Life – Impacts Your Kids:

"Nothing has a stronger influence psychologically on their environment and especially on their children than the unlived life of the parent."

– C.G. Jung

This is something we see far too often amongst second generation Asians entering the UK and US, where there is a quiet weight that unfulfilled lives carry. Not loud, not obvious. But it lingers – in sighs, in silence, in the spaces between what's said and what's meant. When a parent sets aside their dreams, passions, or purpose – believing it noble, necessary, or simply too late – it doesn't vanish. It lingers. And often, it finds its way into the next generation.

Children are more sensitive than we realise. They feel what isn't spoken. They inherit not just our genetics, but our emotional landscapes and insecurities. The unlived life – the book unwritten, the dream unfollowed, the courage never claimed – can quietly become theirs to carry.

But the opposite is also true. When a parent lives with authenticity – imperfect, perhaps, but true to themselves – they give their children something powerful: permission. Permission to live boldly. To try and fail. To value joy over obligation. To know that fulfilment isn't selfish, it's sacred.

So, pursue what lights you up. Heal what dims you. The life you live – or don't – echoes beyond your own.

Getting Old – Living Forward With Intention:

"It's not how old you are, it's how you are old."

– Jules Renard

My last message to my kids – one of the most real and very important:

Getting old is a quiet teacher. It doesn't announce itself all at once, but rather arrives in gentle reminders – a stiff joint here, a forgotten name there. Over time, we realise that ageing is less about the body changing and more about perspective shifting. What once seemed urgent now feels optional. The noise of life begins to quiet, and in its place comes clarity. Time's value increases, but the pressure to fill every moment with productivity fades.

With age comes a strange but steady wisdom: that presence matters more than pace, and peace more than pride. As we enter our 40s and 50s, we juggle careers, ageing parents, and still-young children, while beginning to think about legacy. Just as we become most immersed in life's responsibilities, we start asking about how we want to be remembered and what we hope to leave behind.

Recently, I've been struck by *Die With Zero* by Bill Perkins, a book that challenged my view on legacy and life planning. Perkins suggests a more intentional distribution of resources across time: helping our children at key milestones: college loans, weddings, first homes, and grandchildren.

This kind of financial stewardship – timely, practical, and personal – is more impactful than leaving behind a large estate. It's about living generously and thoughtfully in the present. But while we think about supporting our children, we must also consider the side we often neglect: how we support ourselves as we age.

If we're serious about not being a burden to our kids, that doesn't just happen by chance – it takes planning, honesty, and foresight.

In youth, we focus on accumulating wealth, experience, and reputation. But eventually we must shift gears, prioritising how we live over what we build.

Ageing gracefully isn't just about health or money, it's about alignment. It's ensuring our values, relationships, and lifestyle all support the kind of old age we want, and the person we still hope to become.

If You Knew You Were Going to Die One Year from Today:

Most of us don't like thinking about death. It freaks us out. But thinking about our own death surprisingly has a lot of practical advantages.

One of those advantages is that it forces us to zero in on what's actually important in our lives and what's just frivolous and distracting.

When I was in college, I used to walk around and ask people, "If you had a year to live, what would you do?"

As you can imagine, I was a huge hit at parties. A lot of people gave vague and boring answers. A few drinks were nearly spat on me. But it did cause people to really think about their lives in a different way and re-evaluate what their priorities were.

Ultimately, death is the only thing that gives us perspective on the value of our life. Because it's only by imagining your non-existence that you can get a sense of what is most important about your existence.

What is your legacy going to be? What are the stories people are going to tell when you're gone? What is your obituary going to say? Is there anything to say at all? If not, what would you like it to say? How can you start working towards that today?

When people feel like they have no sense of direction, no purpose in their life, it's because they don't know what's important to them, they don't know what their values are.

How to Stop Ageing:

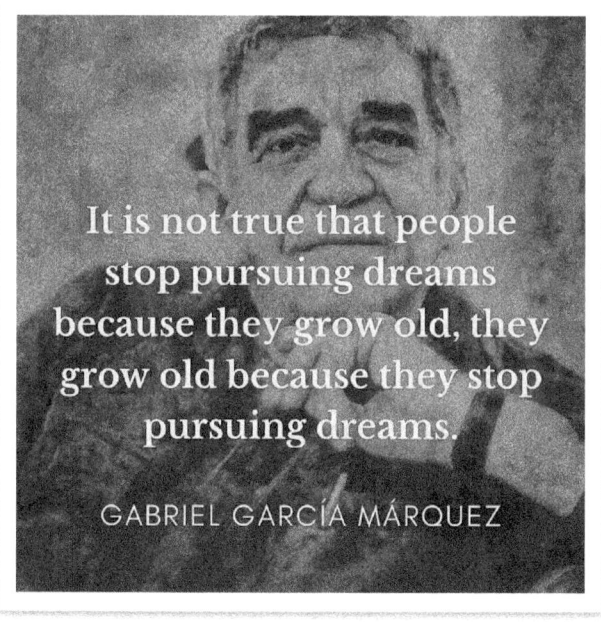

Embrace Life's Unscripted Moments:

> **Life is what happens while you're making other plans.**
> – John Lennon

This deceptively simple and impactful lyric from **Beautiful Boy (Darling Boy)**, written for his son Sean has been at the heart of my philosophy for years. It holds within it a profound truth about human existence. In our relentless pursuit of goals – career ambitions, financial security, perfect relationships – we construct intricate plans, blueprints for a future that we believe we can control. We tell ourselves that life will begin when the plan is complete: after graduation, after the promotion, after the kids grow up, after we retire.

Yet, in the shadow of our forward-looking focus, *life itself unfolds quietly, indifferently, in real time.* The moments that truly shape us – the subtle kindness of a stranger, the heartbreak of a sudden loss, the quiet awe of a sunset – rarely adhere to our schedules. These are not plotted points on a calendar, but spontaneous events that arise in the margins of our intentions.

To say that life "happens" while we plan is not to dismiss the value of planning. Rather, it is a gentle warning: do not mistake the map for the terrain. Plans are necessary – they give direction, structure, even hope. But when we become too consumed by them, we risk becoming spectators of our own lives, forever waiting for the "real" part to begin.

The learning here is both humbling and liberating: *presence* is more vital than control. We must learn to inhabit each moment fully, even when it diverges from our expectations. Life is not a problem to be solved or a project to be completed – it is a mystery to be experienced, in all its glory.

Definition of Happiness:

"If you want to be happy, be."

– Leo Tolstoy

"I love the journey I am on, the texture of my day to day, the diet of people and environment I feed off and the ability to just be intoxicated by being."

True Happiness is the **absence of searching for happiness**. It rejects the idea that I am looking for something, some meaning – and that the ideal is "out there" or "in the future", other than *here*, in this exact moment!

The real goal? **Agency and autonomy over your life.** Agency being the ability to execute things, regardless of the external environment. It gives a person a level of calm confidence that cannot be shaken.

"The problem is that adults stress about everything: their challenges, stress about their successes, stress about being single, stress about being married, stress about not having a job, stress about having a "big" job. It's just never-ending.

Adults have forgotten to enjoy living and few understand the intoxication of just being alive!"

Breathing and being alive should be enough to fill us with gratitude and joy. Everything else is icing on the cake.

Why Does Happiness Elude Successful People?:

The curse of competence states that if you are good at things and have high standards you assume you will always do well – you just expect success in all aspects of life.

Ergo less than success is failure and success is not a cause for celebration but is the minimum threshold of reasonable performance.

You might be very successful but you also may be very miserable!

– Inspired by Chris Williamson, *Modern Wisdom*

Success Is Not What You've Been Told:

What scares me when I talk to people is that they have a dream or a vision but struggle to explain the genesis of it.

Too often they are following someone else's definition of success, and more often than not it's the dream of the parents. Parents are living vicariously through their children.

We're taught to study hard, get a job, work tirelessly, and climb the ladder of success – compete and achieve. But what happens if you find yourself at the top of the ladder, only to realise it was the wrong one?

But let's be honest, real success has nothing to do with how high you climb that ladder, your job title or your bank balance.

It has everything to do with how it feels on the inside. Living a life true to yourself is success.

Inner peace and instilled confidence is success.

I have met too many people in Professional Services, Investment Banking, Private Equity and Tech that live for their title and bank balance. Climbing that ladder is never ending and largely unfulfilling.

The question is what did they abandon to reach those heights.

You can have the title, the income and the praise, yet still feel empty if you have to completely abandon yourself to get there.

Be Truthful to Yourself:

"Above all, don't lie to yourself."

– Fyodor Dostoevsky

A Beautiful Life Includes Hope:

"Hope is the thing with feathers that perches in the soul."

– Emily Dickinson

In this simple yet profound metaphor, Emily Dickinson reveals hope as an eternal presence within us – a delicate yet unwavering force that endures beyond circumstance. Like a bird that sings without asking for reward or recognition, hope dwells quietly in the soul, offering its song amid silence and shadow. It is both fragile and fierce, a testament to the human spirit's capacity to endure and aspire.

Hope does not guarantee ease or certainty, but it sustains the courage to continue, to face each moment with openness and grace. It invites us to embrace life fully, to pursue what stirs our spirit, even as time moves inexorably forward.

Remember: <u>our days are finite – roughly 4,000 weeks</u>, a fleeting measure of existence. This truth calls us not to remain idle in fear or hesitation, but to live with intention and joy. To seek what makes our souls sing and to honour the hope that perches within, urging us onward.

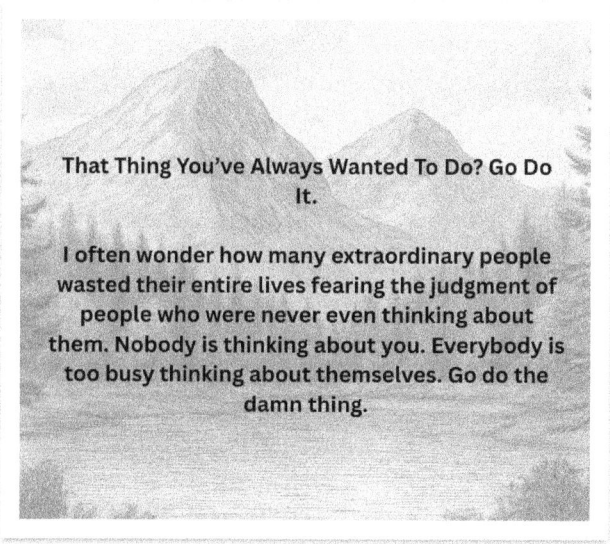

Things Happen When They Are Meant to Happen:

There is a quiet poetry in the belief that everything unfolds when it is meant to – that the universe, in its unseen wisdom, weaves lives together with threads we cannot see.

The Invisible String Theory is such a spiritual thought and at the heart of everything that I believe in. It speaks to this deeper rhythm: that two souls, destined to meet, are kept apart not by cruelty or chance, but by timing that must first ripen. In this view, every detour, heartbreak, delay, or lonely night is not a mistake, but a soft preparation.

Each experience shapes the self into the person capable of recognising, receiving, and cherishing the other. And when that meeting finally comes, it is marked not by grand fanfare, but by a subtle harmony of coincidences too perfect to dismiss.

Had anything shifted – a different city, a missed train, a decision reversed – the moment would have passed like a ghost. Yet it doesn't. Because when it is time, the threads pull tight, and what once felt random reveals itself as necessary.

Fate, then, is not a force of control, but of alignment. It waits, patiently, for readiness.

Showing Up – The Language of True Humanity:

In the face of hardship, true humanity reveals itself not in grand speeches or hesitant offers, but in the simple act of presence.

To show up – without waiting for permission or validation – is to embrace the Stoic virtue of *prohairesis*: the power of our will to act rightly regardless of circumstance.

As Epictetus taught:

> *"First say to yourself what you would be; and then do what you have to do."*

When someone struggles, the question is not whether to ask if they need help, but whether you will embody compassion by standing with them.

Practical kindness requires no proclamation; it is expressed in tangible acts – a meal shared, a message sent, a silent presence beside them. In those moments, showing up is not just kindness; it is a declaration of our shared humanity, a reminder that suffering is not meant to isolate but to connect.

To truly show up is to bridge the distance between souls, to hold space for another's pain without judgement or delay.

It is the quiet courage to act, knowing that sometimes, the most profound support is simply to be there.

> *"People forget what you say, people forget what you do, but they will never forget how you made them feel."*
>
> – Maya Angelou

A Beautiful Life Is Poetry in Motion:

In the quiet moments of our lives, we often speak in simple phrases – words that barely scratch the surface of what we truly feel. "I'm learning to let go," we say, yet the process is far deeper than mere words can capture. It is an unspoken, gentle release of the past, a subtle opening toward new light. These everyday expressions hold layers of longing, loss, and hope, inviting us to look beyond the obvious and discover the poetry woven through the rhythms of our hearts.

In everyday words, we say, "I'm learning to let go."

But true letting go is a quiet unburdening – our hands releasing the past to welcome the future's light.

We say, "I miss the way things used to be."

Yet beneath this, we search for lost colours on a canvas that time slowly fades to grey.

We say, "I dream about you."

But dreams are petals unfolding softly, revealing truths that dawn alone can touch.

We say, "You don't love me anymore."

Yet love's absence is like a closed door – silent, unyielding, and impossible to enter.

"To live beautifully is to see the poetry beneath the plain words, to feel deeply the unspoken rhythms of life."

Learning to Die Peacefully:

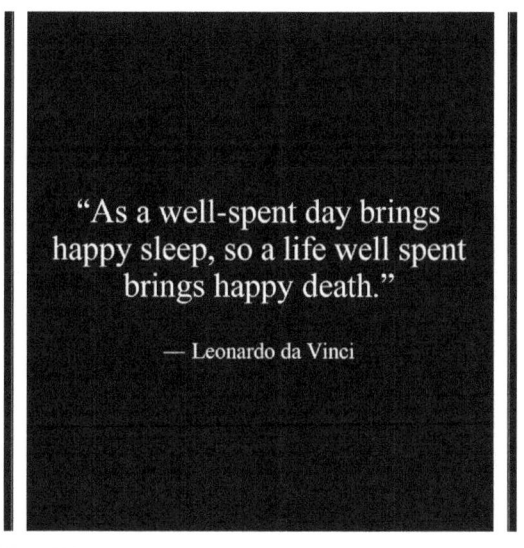

www.ingramcontent.com/pod-product-compliance
Lightning Source LLC
Chambersburg PA
CBHW060539010526
44119CB00053B/762